KINGDOMS AT WAR

KINGDOMS AT WAR

BILL BRIGHT & RON JENSON

Here's Life Publishers

Published by
Here's Life Publishers, Inc.
P.O. Box 1576
San Bernardino, CA 92402

Library of Congress Cataloging in Publication Data
Bright, Bill.
    Kingdoms at war.
    Bibliography: p.
    1. Christianity—United States.   2. Humanism—
20th century.   3. United States—Moral conditions.
4. Church and social problems—United States.
I. Jenson, Ron.   II. Title.
BR526.B65   1986   209'.73   85-5858
ISBN 0-86605-160-0 (pbk.)

FOR MORE INFORMATION, WRITE:

L.I.F.E.—P.O. Box A399, Sydney South 2000, Australia
Campus Crusade for Christ of Canada—Box 368, Abbotsford, B.C., V25 4N9, Canada
Campus Crusade for Christ—103 Friar Street, Reading RGl IEP, Berkshire, England
Lay Institute for Evangelism—P.O. Box 8786, Auckland 3, New Zealand
Great Commission Movement of Nigeria—P.O· Box 500, Jos, Plateau State Nigeria, West Africa
Campus Crusade for Christ International—Arrowhead Springs, San Bernardino, CA 92414, U.S.A.

THIRD PRINTING, JUNE 1988

For he has rescued us out of
the darkness and gloom of
Satan's kingdom and brought us
into the kingdom of his dear
Son, who bought our freedom
with his blood and forgave us
all our sins.

Colossians 1:13-14
The Living Bible

Acknowledgments

Someone has said that writing a book is like giving birth. We do not believe it. Oh, we do not mean to say that it is harder, but it is a much longer process. We are sure the pain is not nearly so great—obviously, we have not really experienced the pain of childbirth. But we know that it has taken a great deal of work to get this book in your hands.

Consider getting together two men who do not like to sit still in the first place to conceptualize a book. Then imagine coordinating schedules for two men who travel extensively, even overseas a great deal. Then imagine the chore of getting two independent men to do something like this together.

We want to acknowledge those who helped to make this book possible. First, we thank our personal staffs—Erma Griswold, Tim Bolen, Ed Taflinger, Mary Banks, Charlene Elston and a host of others who helped us stay on schedule.

Next we thank our supportive wives, Vonette and Mary, who constantly support, critique, challenge and complete us.

We are grateful for those who read the manuscript and gave valuable feedback, including Zachary Bright, Paul Cox, Mark McCloskey and Herbert Schlossberg. We are thankful also for those who helped edit the manuscript, including Les Stobbe, Jean Bryant, Kirby Anderson, Carol Crawford, John Jones, and especially Al Janssen, who helped with the initial draft of the book. His helpful counsel, input, drafting and initial writing were exceedingly helpful.

We are especially appreciative of the team at the Public Policy Resource Center (PPRC) for their assistance in research, interaction, rewriting, typing and editing. Al Dunham and Jay Davis thoroughly followed up on research and, together with Roy Hanson, developed the excellent bibliography and some of the appendixes. Kim Simpkins and Evelyn Foster were supportive in giving attention to the details.

We especially thank Roy Hanson for his tireless persistence in follow-through and coordination of this project. Without his help these two entrepreneurs would have never finished—at least not in this millennium.

A final word of appreciation must go to the One who impressed us to write this book, which we believe needed urgently to be written, and who by His grace and wisdom gave us the able associates to help make it available to you.

Bill Bright
Ron Jenson

Table of Contents

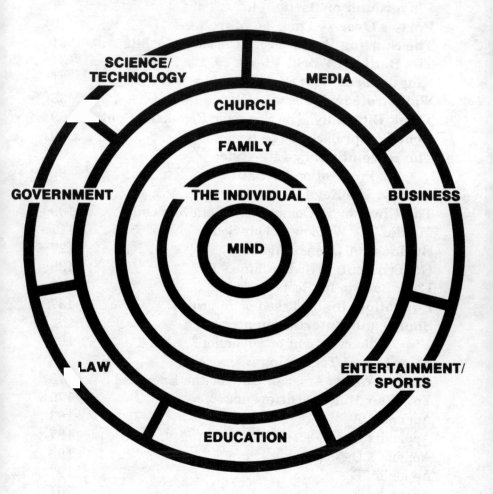

1

PLAYGROUND OR BATTLEFIELD?

I magine a world in which healthy, active citizens are automatically put to death at age seventy five; where the law limits each married couple to a single child; where physicians are assigned by the state to their patients, and commissioned not to heal the sick, but to weed out the diseased from society; where cameras and secret microphones track the moves and conversations of ordinary citizens.

No, we are not talking about the U.S.S.R.—or any other totalitarian country. We are discussing a future United States, as portrayed in the frightening novel *Winterflight*,[1] by Joe Bayly.

Bayly centers his plot on a young Christian couple who discover that their son has hemophilia (normal blood-clotting factors are absent, causing prolonged bleeding from even minor cuts and injuries). They dare not seek medical help for him, because they know that victims of chronic diseases, when discovered, are terminated by the state and their bodies kept on life support so that their organs may be harvested for "healthy people."

The couple cannot even have certain trust in other members of their church congregation—each church must be registered with the state, and so could be full of spies.

Dissidents who fight the system, such as the doctor who tries to help them, find themselves in prison camp in Alaska.

And the United States government has become so sensitive to Third World opinion that it has stopped issuing passports to missionaries who wish to work there.

The situation forces Bayly's protagonists to consider fleeing the country or pursuing other extreme alternatives in order to remain true to their Christianity. Bayly paints a picture almost too bleak to contemplate.

Many believe such a scenario will be an inevitable reality if present trends continue. But it need not come about, if ordinary people will commit themselves to restoring Christian values to our society. You can make a difference. Consider the following examples.

A Victory Over Globalism

The National Association of Christian Educators has, for some time, been carefully monitoring the Global Education movement. This movement's proponents attempt to instill in children a planetary loyalty, which overrides loyalties to God, family or country. So strongly do they believe in their Global Village that they have labeled patriotism as mental illness!

Recently, a bill was introduced in Washington State to implement a Global Education program in their public schools. The legislation received backing from the American Humanist Association, the American Civil Liberties Union (ACLU), the National Education Association and the American Atheists Association. The bill looked like it would pass easily until a Washington pastor, John Wilson, began to speak against it.

The bill did pass in the legislature by a narrow vote and then moved on to the Ways and Means Committee for funding. At that point Pastor Wilson, along with Dr. Robert Simonds and others from the National Association of Christian Educators, put together a plea for help and mailed it to concerned Christians and churches all over the state. The letter enjoyed great response, resulting in a flood of calls and telegrams to the capitol.

The legislators were so impressed that they allowed the bill to die in committee.

One pastor, one letter, and the concern of many ordinary people brought about this vital change in the educational future of a state full of school children.[2]

The Arthur S. DeMoss Foundation

Trying to reach the masses with the message of Christ over the din of humanistic media programming can seem impossible. Yet, during the "Year of the Bible," 1983, the DeMoss Foundation decided to offer a free copy of the book, *Power for Living,* nationwide. This book was written to provide biblical answers to the challenges and problems people face in everyday life and to demonstrate that the ultimate answer to life is Jesus Christ.

The well-prepared television spots and written materials obviously touched a nerve in magazine readers' and television viewers' hearts, because the campaign brought in more than eleven million requests for copies of this life-changing book.

The Foundation followed that with a 1986 television special, "America, You're Too Young to Die." This special was conceived and produced by a young woman from the Foundation, in her early twenties, who had a burden to see her world changed.

Her powerful documentary traces how we, as a nation, have drifted from the Christian influences that made our nation strong, prosperous and healthy. It offers a challenge to Americans to return to God and His standards in order to restore America. It aired in a hundred cities, again offering a free book to viewers. More than one-and-a-half million requests by mail and telephone have reconfirmed the public's hunger for God's answers to the deep questions of life.[3]

The Foundation, established by one committed businessman, has become his family's resource for several national, evangelistic and revival efforts that are helping to change America.

The National Federation for Decency

Penthouse and *Playboy* are not as healthy as they used to be,[4] thanks, in part, to the Reverend Don Wildmon and the organization he heads, the National Federation for Decency. The November 1985 NFD Journal reported that the two magazines themselves attributed serious drops in circulation to the efforts of the NFD.

This organization encourages its members and supporters to boycott retail establishments that sell pornography. It has also set up campaigns in which members phone the chairmen of offending companies to express their concerns.

Their results are impressive. They cite 7,000 stores across the nation who have decided "to get out of the porn business."[5] Among them are several national names and many regional ones including: The Kroger Company,[6] Albertsons Food Stores,[7] QuikTrip convenience stores in Oklahoma, Convenient Food Mart in Ohio, and many more. Even the 7-Eleven stores, owned by Southland Corporation of Dallas, have announced that they will no longer carry these magazines. Today, because one man cared enough to start a movement,[8] far fewer sources exist for obtaining the deviant material that does such harm to families.

The Rutherford Institute

Who represents Christians in the courts when confronted by well-heeled ACLU lawyers? The Rutherford Institute, directed by attorney and author John Whitehead, has pledged itself to protect the rights of Christians who face harassment because of their beliefs, and in recent years the Institute has had more than enough work to do.

One of its cases concerned Florida neonatal nurse Sandra Tosti, who found herself on duty while a seventeen-ounce baby was being denied standard care because it was the survivor of a botched abortion.

Horrified, she telephoned her prayer partner during

her dinner break and asked for prayer for the child's life. Through other sources, news of the incident began to spread through the hospital and to the public. Sandra Tosti was blamed for the news leak and was consequently fired.

The Rutherford Institute aided her in filing a civil action against the hospital, alleging religious discrimination, wrongful and retaliatory discharge and breach of contract. The suit was later voluntarily dismissed. Institute general counsel for this case, Thomas Neuberger, said that the case "will send a message to hospitals throughout the country that they cannot ride roughshod over the sincerely held beliefs of Christians."[9]

In a second case, two news reporters were arrested for criminal trespass after they covered a pro-life sit-in at a Delaware abortion clinic. As the reporters, who happened to be pro-life, were banished from the building, a *Cosmopolitan* reporter was given carte blanche to cover the incident. The Rutherford Institute staff assisted the two reporters, Louis Johnson and Daniel Menefee of WNNN radio in Canton, New Jersey, in gaining an acquittal on the grounds that insufficient evidence existed that a crime had been committed.[10]

Many of the battles for preserving traditional values will take place in the courts in days to come. To win them, the combatants will need skilled legal assistance such as that offered by the Rutherford Institute.

Concerned Women for America

In a truly remarkable response to the agitation of the National Organization of Women (NOW), Beverly LaHaye has founded an organization, Concerned Women for America (CWA), to represent the concerns of Christian women who do not share the views of such groups as NOW.

Recently, CWA's general counsel, Michael Farris, represented a group of Tennessee parents in an important constitutional battle with their school district. These parents filed suit in December, 1983, after the school district expelled some of their children for refusing to read textbooks that violated the religious beliefs of the families.

The parents found much objectionable material in the books, including situation ethics, presentations on witchcraft, and attempted discrediting of biblical documents. At first, their complaint was dismissed, but an appeals court reversed that decision and ordered the case to trial. The parents credit their CWA lawyers for keeping open the possibility of victory.[11]

In another case, CWA helped to defend a blind student who qualified for vocational rehabilitation benefits from the state of Washington but was denied them when the state learned that he wanted to study for the ministry. Larry Witters had planned to attend Inland School of the Bible in Spokane and study to be a minister, missionary or youth worker. The state held the position that such an educational goal violated the separation of church and state.

The Supreme Court has agreed to hear the case, but the decision has not been reached as of this writing.[12]

Obviously, Concerned Women for America also fulfills a need for a strong and skilled response to situations where believers find their rights called into question.

Christians in Broadcast Media

To reach people in a technological age, we need to use technological tools. Two organizations which use them particularly well are the Christian Broadcasting Network and James Dobson's ministry, Focus on the Family.

CBN now reports a $233 million annual income, according to the February 17, 1986, *Time* magazine. The article cites a 1984 University of Pennsylvania survey estimating that "13.3 million people, or 6.2 percent of the national TV audience, are regular viewers . . ."[13] Even more impressive, a Nielsen survey in 1985 showed that "21% of the nation's TV households tune in to Christian TV."[14]

James Dobson has used his radio programs and films

to reach millions of people with helpful information on preserving and strengthening the family. In fact, his film series, *Focus on the Family,* has reached fifty million people. He produced this first series in order to "help families around the world without taking on a heavy travel schedule that would disrupt his own home life,"[15] according to *Focus on the Family* magazine.

Now he is offering a second series called *Turn Your Heart Toward Home.* These films will touch a number of responsive chords in viewers' lives, as they deal with topics such as priorities, guilt and power in parent-child relationships, public policy's effect on the family, and current family issues such as pornography. The series also includes a touching testimony by Dr. Dobson's wife, Shirley, about her painful childhood.

In another outreach directly aimed at men who are heads of families, Dr. Dobson has offered a videotape called *Where's Dad?* for television viewing in communities around the country. These videotapes target men who do not normally attend church but might watch a television program on God's plan for families. General John A. Wickham, Jr., U.S. Army Chief of Staff, gave his strong personal endorsement to the tape which has been distributed to army posts around the world.[16]

Conclusion

These examples make it clear. Much can be done by individual people who commit themselves, in obedience to God, to making a difference in our world and our nation.

The next five to ten years are critical! We can begin to restore moral sanity to this country, if we put ourselves to work now. The alternative is to remain silent and watch the plagues depicted in *Winterflight* continue to come upon us all.

The anti-Christian forces have already gained much ground.

2

PARTY'S OVER— TIME TO MARCH

In the late 1970s, Harvey and Jenny Pflug were concerned about the slow, sporadic growth of their four-year-old son, Danny. They took him to several doctors, who ran batteries of tests to try to determine the cause of his stunted growth. Finally, with the help of nutritional therapy, Danny began to grow again.

About that time a state social worker investigated. He determined that the boy's well-being was endangered by the Christian views and practices of the parents and ordered him committed to a hospital for testing and therapy. Thus began a one year ordeal as the parents fought to regain legal custody of their son.[1]

More and more parents like the Pflugs are having their children removed by zealous social workers determined to "protect" children from their Christian parents. But that is not the only threat to freedom. Churches are looking over their shoulders as "big brother" intrudes on the practice of religion.

On April 1, 1979, twenty-four-year-old Kenneth Nally put a shotgun to his head and ended his troubled life. One year later, his parents filed a malpractice suit against Grace Community Church in Sun Valley, California, claiming that the counseling he received was responsible for their son's death. At first, Judge Thomas Murphy in Superior Court of Los Angeles County stated that he could see "no triable case at this particular time."

But a three-judge Appeals Court bench ruled the case could go to court on an entirely different basis than that raised by the plaintiffs. In a split decision, it was ruled that "a reasonable inference could be drawn...that Grace Community Church and each of the individual defendants...followed a policy of counseling suicidal persons that, if one was unable to overcome one's sins, suicide was an acceptable and even desirable alternative to living." That inference was erroneously based on a one-minute excerpt taken out of context from a twelve-hour lecture series on counseling taped eighteen months after the suicide.[2] The church pastors say they have always taught that suicide is a sin, and have never counseled anyone to view it as a way of dealing with sin.

In another case, Marian Guinn, an Oklahoma woman, won a $390,000 judgment against the Collinsville Church of Christ for publicly rebuking her before the church membership concerning the sin of fornication. The church believed it was following the biblically prescribed steps for discipline as described in Matthew 18:17. The jury, however, agreed with Marian Guinn's claim that, as a single woman in America, whatever she did with her body was her own business, not the church's.[3]

We can move into the schools and find many more examples of the systematic assault on religious freedoms. In some schools, teachers are forbidden to meet for Bible study before starting their school day. In one high school in Minnesota, students were suspended for distributing a Christian newspaper to their friends. A Christian school in Nebraska was closed and padlocked by officials because it refused to submit to state control.

The cancer of destructive forces against traditional values has invaded the medical profession, with life and death implications. Abortions were once universally condemned by the medical profession. Now they are performed routinely.

James Watson, the man who, along with Francis

Crick, cracked the DNA genetic code, has already suggested the next logical step. "Most birth defects are not discovered until birth. If a child were not declared alive until three days after birth, then all parents could be allowed the choice...the doctor could allow the child to die if the parents so choose and save a lot of misery and suffering."[4] Some of Watson's colleagues feel three days is too soon. Some suggest thirty days after birth. Others suggest a minimum I.Q. measurement as qualification to live.

The cancer has spread to virtually every profession. Much of the news and entertainment media routinely ridicule God-fearing people while elevating the pleasures of self-gratification. Many businesspeople place profit ahead of moral integrity. Newspapers tell of judges making public policy decisions based on public or personal opinion rather than on the Constitution.

Where Did We Start?

By contrast, let us look back over the philosophies, people and events that have shaped America over the past three hundred years. Most of our present history books have been rewritten in such a way that they fail to record the Judeo-Christian influence that affected the formation of this nation.

For example, none of the first colonial colleges was founded as a secular institution. They were all Christian in their orientation, and eight of the first nine colleges were specifically founded for the purpose of training students for Christian ministry. America's first college, Harvard, had as its 1636 motto, "For Christ and the Church," and its primary purpose was "the education of English and Indian youths...in all good literature and Godlynes."[5] Rutgers, originally named Queen's College, was established "For the Education of the Youth...in true Religion and useful Learning, and particularly for providing an able and learned Protestant Ministry."[6]

George Washington was among those of our early leaders who unashamedly honored and feared God. It is

"HEY, NO PRAYING HERE... THIS IS A PUBLIC BEACH !"

reported that for many years of his adult life, it was his custom to begin and end every day on his knees in Bible reading and prayer.[7]

One of the most striking evidences of the thinking of our founding fathers occurred during the Constitutional Convention in 1787. Debate and disagreement had become increasingly bitter, and the convention threatened to collapse. Then Benjamin Franklin, a man not particularly known for his religious convictions, rose and reminded the men of something they had forgotten in the heat of controversy.

> "I have lived...a long time, and the longer I live, the more convincing proofs I see of this truth: 'that God governs in the affairs of men.' And if a sparrow cannot fall to the ground without His notice, is it probable that an empire can rise without His aid?...I therefore beg leave to move that, henceforth, prayers imploring the assistance of heaven and its blessing on our deliberation, be held in this assembly every morning before we proceed to business."[8]

Thomas Jefferson, third President of the United States, was not known as a Christian, yet he wrote, "The God who gave us life, gave us liberty at the same time."[9] He also wrote, "Can the liberties of a nation be thought secure, when we have removed their only firm basis, a conviction in the minds of the people that these liberties are the gifts of God?"[10]

Acknowledgment of God's sovereignty, guidance and protection of this nation, with its unique history, did not end with the colonial period. President Abraham Lincoln, during one of the darkest moments in our history, proclaimed a national day of prayer and fasting at the initiative of the United States Senate. The proclamation stated in part, ". . . Devoutly recognizing the Supreme authority and just government of Almighty God in all of the affairs of men and nations, has by a resolution, requested the President to designate and set apart a day for national prayer and humiliation."[11]

In 1892, the Supreme Court made an exhaustive study of the supposed connection between Christianity and the United States government and concluded "that this is a religious people...a Christian nation."[12] In 1931, Justice George Sutherland reiterated that Americans were a "Christian people." And in 1952, Justice William O. Douglas affirmed in the case of *Zorach vs. Clauson*: "We are a religious people, and our institutions presuppose a Supreme Being."[13]

President Woodrow Wilson declared, "America was born a Christian nation. America was born to exemplify that devotion to the elements of righteousness which are derived from the revelations of Holy Scripture."[14] President Calvin Coolidge, commenting on the influential role of biblical principles in the life of our nation, said, "The

" I ONLY PRAYED 53 SECONDS THIS MORNING ... COULD I
USE THE OTHER 7 NOW ? "

foundations of our society and of our government rest so much on the teachings of the Bible, that it would be difficult to support them, if faith in these teachings should cease to be practically universal in this country."[15]

Don't Build a House Without a Foundation

Throughout most of our nation's history, we have acknowledged that ours is a country blessed by God. Yet, in recent years we seem to have forgotten that truth. We do so at our own peril.

Before the Israelites entered the promised land, Moses spoke these words: "If you fully obey all of these commandments of the LORD your God [including the Ten Commandments]...God will transform you into the greatest nation in the world....The LORD will defeat your enemies before you....The LORD will bless you with good crops and healthy cattle, and prosper everything you do....All the nations in the world shall see that you belong to the LORD, and they will stand in awe....If you won't listen to the LORD your God and won't obey these laws... then all of these curses shall come upon you."[16]

These passages were spoken and written specifically for the nation of Israel. However, the principles they express apply to any nation.[17] For much of our national history, we have applied these principles and have experienced great blessing.

A gradual change has taken place since the second half of the 19th century, however. Probably most symbolic of the change in our nation's attitude was the 1963 Supreme Court decision in the case of *Abington Township vs. Schempp*. This ruling had the effect of virtually banishing prayer and all mention of God from the public schools, even though the decision itself did not explicitly call for this. In 1983, the President's Commission on Education reported that education in America "began to disintegrate 20 years ago." But no reference was made to this 1963 Supreme Court ruling.

A careful reading of Deuteronomy, especially chapters 8 and 28, teaches that the blessing of God comes

when people remember God and keep His commandments. The people who forget God will incur His judgment. From our perspective, this Supreme Court decision
was in direct violation of God's Word, and helps explain
one major reason our nation's educational system is in
trouble.

What happened in the years following the Supreme
Court decision might well be interpreted as modern-day
"plagues" sent by God in His providence to chasten our
nation. Shortly after that decision, President Kennedy
was assassinated. One might argue that this was only a
coincidence. But in following years there were also the
assassinations of Senator Robert F. Kennedy and the Reverend Martin Luther King, Jr. In the mid-60s, the conflict
in Vietnam began to accelerate, and before it was over,
more than 55,000 American men lost their lives. Our
nation began a period of self-doubt.

Here at home, the drug culture swept millions of
young men and women into addiction, and many millions
more became alcoholics. Racial conflict erupted in numerous cities. Crime rates skyrocketed. The Watergate scan-
dal eroded trust in government leadership. The homes of
our land continued to disintegrate even more rapidly,
with soaring divorce rates and pregnancies among unwed
teenagers reaching epidemic proportions. The increasing
institutional care of dependent family members, both
young (in day care centers) and old (in nursing homes)
further threatened the solidarity of the traditional family.[18] Suicide became a leading cause of death among
young people.

The public schools themselves were in a downhill
slide. Scholastic Aptitude Test scores declined steadily
from 1963 to 1980. There was a dramatic upsurge in van-
dalism against school properties and violence against
both students and teachers, with one result being that
millions of concerned parents transferred their children
to private schools.

Alarmed at the downward spiral of our national life,
on April 29, 1980, some 500,000 Christians of all races
and backgrounds gathered in Washington, D.C., to hum-

ble themselves before God, to fast and pray and ask His forgiveness and cleansing of our land. Since that day there has been much evidence that God heard our prayer and is changing our country. President Reagan and both houses of Congress proclaimed 1983 the "Year of the Bible." Could God be hearing us and healing our land? In the following months, our economy made a dramatic turnaround, employment rose, and inflation rates, crime rates and even divorce rates began to fall.

We do not want to sound foolishly optimistic. There is much more that needs God's redemptive work. We acknowledge the continuing increase of reported child abuse and sexual assaults, 1.5 million abortions each year, the continued breakdown of the family, the ballooning national debt, the spread of Acquired Immune Deficiency Syndrome (AIDS) primarily among homosexuals, and the growth of communist influence below our southern borders. Certainly our nation has terrible troubles, which will persist unless God continues a gracious work in its behalf.

We believe God wants to bless our land, for this is the one nation founded by people who desired to glorify Him and who believed the principles found in His Word. We believe God wants to bless our land because it is the major bastion of freedom[19] of speech, the press, religion and economics; standing against the forces of slavery, atheism and tyranny. We believe God wants to bless our land because America is the primary source of funding and personnel for the unprecedented spread of the gospel throughout the world.[20]

But we are a long way from regaining the full blessings that this nation once enjoyed. Too many Christians have become self-centered, materialistic, undisciplined and committed to little more than their own fleshly pleasures. They give little thought to their responsibilities before God.

Revolution Now

What we need is a revolution. One dictionary defines

a revolution as "a complete or drastic change of any kind."[21] Many may cringe at that term, for historically, revolution has been associated with violence. We are *not* calling for change by using violent or manipulative means to force opinions on people. We *are* talking about a dramatic change in our society, a change brought about by committed Christian men and women who are willing to dedicate their lives to helping this nation return to its biblical and moral roots.

This is a call for radical change in the way we conduct business, run our government, write our laws, care for the sick, communicate in the news media, entertain the masses, educate our children, raise our families and conduct our churches. We believe we are engaged in a war—not a conventional war fought with guns and bombs, but an ideological war, a battle for the mind of every American, old and young alike.

Many believe they are powerless to fight in this war. They have already given up. Others want to enter the battle but do not know what to do. Nineteenth-century evangelist Dwight L. Moody once heard someone say, "The world has yet to see what God can do in and through a man who is fully and wholly consecrated to Him."[22] We believe that a few men and women so dedicated and scattered throughout each of the major professions can radically influence their disciplines and our country for good.

Diagram 1 illustrates our approach to this book. We are engaged in a warfare of ideas. The impact of that warfare has an ever-widening influence on the mind, on the individual, on the family, in the church, and in the various professions. We are under attack in each area, and the battle must be waged on many fronts.

This warfare is particularly seen in the classroom and the media, which are, in many cases, increasingly secular and anti-God. But strategic, foundational areas must be addressed first. For instance, we might win the battle in one area of the media, such as slowing down pornography. However, if the church, the Body of Christ, does not become healthier and stronger, we cannot sustain this change. A healthy local church will produce healthy

Diagram 1

Patterns of Influence

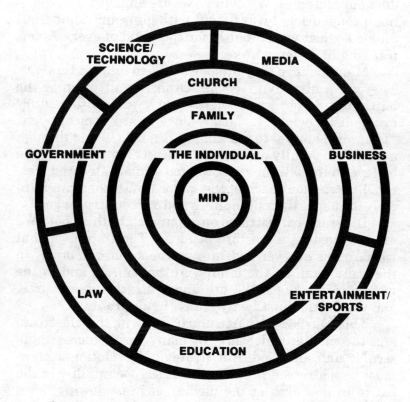

professionals, who will sustain ministries targeted to continue the battle against pornography. Furthermore, churches cannot be changed in a sustained way until the family is changed,and the family's health is determined by the individual's health and personal holiness, which begins in the heart and mind of each one of us.

Too often, we Christians fail to see the larger battle of ideas. We either retreat to narrow, pietistic church huddles; or we become a part of the narcissistic, materialistic world culture. We typically see only one or two issues as important enough to get excited about.

As the late Francis Schaeffer said in the opening words of his classic, *A Christian Manifesto*:

> The basic problem of the Christians in the last eighty years or so ... is that they have seen things in bits and pieces instead of totals.[23]

The real battle is over who is in charge, who will rule and what is our final authority for life in this world. Either God is in charge or man is. Either God is sovereign or man is. Either God's Word is our final authority or man's opinions, experiences and reasonings are. There is no neutral ground. You serve either God's kingdom or Satan's kingdom.

There are many wonderful people who are a part of Satan's kingdom who would be horrified to discover that fact. When properly informed, they would want to join with Christ and His kingdom. Most of the members of Satan's kingdom of darkness do not know that they are serving him. They often consider that they are only "doing their own thing," though they are admittedly self-centered.

To understand how we can turn the tide of this war, we need to go to the starting point—one man with an idea.

Summary

- There are destructive, anti-biblical forces at work in our country.
- The founding fathers of the United States displayed a trust in God and His Word when developing the Con-

stitution and laws of our country.
- Rejection of God's moral standards resulted in "plagues" on this country.
- A return to God, a "revolution" of repentance, can help return our nation to a place worthy of God's blessing.

ACTION STEP

Ask yourself: Am I part of the problem or part of the solution?

As you continue to read, you will discover how you can help change our world!

3

THE STARTING POINT:

Every Christian Counts

One person *can* make a difference.

Eighteenth-century England was in many ways similar to 20th-century America. The moral fiber of society had deteriorated until it was common for high society men to spend more time with their mistresses than with their own wives. Gambling pervaded many of the clubs and pubs.

One of Britain's leading industries was the slave trade. While slavery was not practiced inside the borders of England, at least 160 British ships were involved in securing and transporting slaves from Africa to various colonies. The industry employed some 5,500 men and generated millions of pounds for the economy.

How could one man fight such powerful social, political and economic forces? One man, strategically placed, did just that. His name was William Wilberforce, a distinguished member of Parliament and close friend of Prime Minister William Pitt.

Wilberforce was a recognized member of London society, a bachelor who enjoyed all the sensual pleasures that his culture had to offer. But a tremendous change occurred in his life, as a result of a spiritual renewal spurred by the preaching of John Wesley and George

Whitefield. It was then that he began the habit of starting each day in Bible study and prayer, and that daily time with God began to revolutionize his life.

As a result of his Christian convictions, Wilberforce began a long battle to abolish slave trade and reform the nation's social "manners." Garth Lean wrote about Wilberforce in his book, *Brave Men Choose*:

> Wilberforce believed that these national manners must change if the country was to remain great. His first step had been to change his own ways. Up till then those few society people who had been affected by Wesley had been written off as cranks, but this could not quite be done with Pitt's best friend and one of the ablest speakers in the House. His uncompromising-but-courteous attitude caused many to think. Like Pitt they could not combat the correctness of his thinking "if Christianity be true." Being nominal Christians, they were strangely vulnerable to the challenge that they should live what they professed.[1]

Wilberforce was persistent in his fights. For eighteen of twenty years, he introduced legislation to abolish slave trade in the British Empire. For his efforts, Wilberforce endured abuse, character assassination, even threats on his life. Few could have withstood the attacks, yet in 1807, the abolition of slave trade was finally achieved.

The legacy of this one man was a renewed vitality in a great nation. Lean explains:

> First, he brought a new climate to British political life....Wilberforce and his friends, in particular, pioneered political integrity in an age of corruption and began a tradition, only now being questioned, that self-restraint and the ability to build a sound home are important qualifications for anyone who aspires to lead a nation.
>
> Secondly, Wilberforce and his colleagues did much to shape and inform Britain's main gift to the world, parliamentary democracy...
>
> Lastly, there is Wilberforce's legacy to Africa....But for his work the whole of Africa must have been converted into a vast slave Empire....
>
> Wilberforce lived that higher statesmanship which consists in executing a divine plan—a plan which is always available for statesmen, as for ordinary men, but which has to be actively sought and obeyed.[2]

How can one man make such a difference?

Have an Idea Worth Fighting For

Our society exists today because of ideas. In 1859, Charles Darwin published his book *The Origin of Species*, which detailed his theory that all of life evolved through the process of natural selection from simple, common life forms. Today, his theory is accepted by many as scientific fact and has been applied to form the basis of much of our social philosophy.

John Maynard Keynes was the man most responsible for the ideas that led to Franklin Roosevelt's New Deal. His theory was that government should provide employment through public works, rather than relying on a free economy to solve economic problems. His plan led to government debt as a way of stimulating the economy, with the result that, today, our own government spends billions more than it takes in. The official debt of the United States government is more than *one trillion* dollars, with more than ten trillion dollars in additional unfunded liabilities. Indeed, the largest budget item will be to pay the interest owed by our indebted government.[3]

At this point, the government is borrowing more than half of all new savings in America—over $100 billion dollars a year. In the 1960s the government borrowed only 4 percent of all new savings; in the '70s, 25 percent.

In the '80s, the amount has risen to 50 percent of all the money available for investment in the United States.[4]

We could cite many other examples of ideas that have changed the world: John Dewey's theory of modern education made schools agents of social change rather than communicators of truth; Soren Kierkegaard's existentialism influenced modern Protestant theology; Sigmund Freud was the father of modern psychology; physicist Albert Einstein's theory of relativity propelled us into the space age. Nothing results from a vacuum. Ideas determine every action.

In the prologue to his book *In Search of History*, Theodore H. White, writing in third person, explained why he re-examined politics late in his life:

> Identities in politics, he now realized, were connected far more to ideas than to ego, to id, or to glands. At the core of every great political identity lay an idea—an idea imposed on the leader from his past, which the leader absorbed, changed and then imposed on the others outside....But the idea that *ideas* counted, that ideas were the beginning of all politics, was now, when he was sixty, pressing his thinking back to his adolescence. The men he had since reported in politics were all of them the vessels of ideas. The armies, the navies, the budgets, the campaign organizations they commanded flowed from the ideas that shaped them, or the ideas they could transmit and enforce. Whether it was Mao and Chou, or Nixon and Haldeman, or Kennedy and McNamara, or De Gaulle and Monnet, their identities came from the ideas that had been pumped into them, the ideas they chose in turn to pump out. Their cruelties and nobilities, their creations and tragedies, flowed far more certainly from what was in their minds than from what was in their glands.[5]

Ideas Originate From a Person's World View

What is a world view? It is a mental blueprint or map, an organizing grid or model used to interpret and explain reality and to guide in moral decisions. Everyone has a world view, whether or not he is aware of it, or whether or not it is highly developed.

Our world view is both dynamic and static. It is dynamic in that it is continually being formulated, but it is static in that we constantly use it to explain our existence, to give order to the world in which we live, and to guide our decisions. The challenge we face is to acquire a world view that adequately answers basic questions such as: What is real? Who is man? What is the basis of morality? What is the meaning of human history? The next chapter, "The Battle of World Views," gives a more complete explanation of this concept.

Many factors contribute to our world view, including peer pressure, our parents, our education, the mass media, the Bible, the church and other forces. Our world view may be conscious or unconscious, but it shapes our destiny and affects the destiny of the society in which we live.

Many times we develop a portion of our world view in response to an incident in which we feel a need to justify our own behavior or attitude. At other times we attempt to explain the world as it appears to us. Few are even aware of what a world view is and its importance. Fewer still take the time to think through and adopt a complete and consistent world view. The key question is not so much how we develop our world view, but how we determine which world view is right.

You have heard it said, "Ideas have consequences." We agree. Notice the impact of Islam and Marxism. These ideas have captivated hundreds of millions. As Diagram 2 illustrates, an *idea* strikes the *leaders*, who influence the *masses*, with the result that the whole *world* is changed because of an idea.

We are convinced Christianity is the truth that should have a substantial impact throughout the whole world. We, as Christians, must be prepared to show those who do not have a biblical world view that their world view is inadequate—that it does not adequately fit reality or properly and consistently answer the questions of life.

Ideas Produce Revolutions

Two revolutions of the 17th and 18th centuries illustrate the impact of world view thinking. One resulted in unwarranted chaos and violence. The other was primarily an orderly and peaceful change.

Diagram 2

Ideas Have Consequences

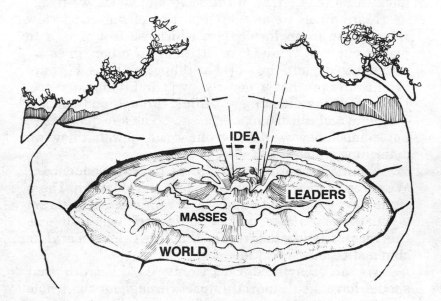

The French Revolution, an event in the period of the Enlightenment, resulted in the senseless loss of many lives and a turbulent restructuring of French society. It was the logical conclusion for those enamored with man's independent reason. The chief proponents of the French part of the Enlightenment were Voltaire and Jean Jacques Rousseau. Both men had elevated human reason to be the supreme standard by which all things were to be governed. They believed that through purely rational and scientific means man could eventually reach perfection. All this was predicated on the idea that man was basically good.

The French Revolution was the culmination of a world view grounded in the belief that man was and should be an independent, autonomous being, his own ruler and not subject to any higher being or higher law. This led to the idea that law should be determined solely by the will of a majority of the people, who, they believed, were accountable only to themselves. Therefore, when it became the general or majority will of the people to change their law and government, they began a bloody revolution. This led to waves of chaos and anarchy, which in turn led to a succession of totalitarian leaders eventually culminating in the rise of Napoleon.

By contrast, the seed of a different kind of revolution was germinated in the mind of a German monk named Martin Luther. The Reformation restored the supremacy of God and His Word as the reliable standard for determining the law of the land. As well, John Calvin in Geneva influenced many in the Protestant Reformation to give God's Word the preeminence it deserves. Those who led the American War of Independence were influenced more by the ideas of the Reformation than they were by the ideas of the Enlightenment.

Coupled with the Reformation's view of God and His Word being the ultimate standard for all law was another idea coming out of a 1644 book by Samuel Rutherford, *Lex Rex,* or, *The Law and the Prince.* Rutherford challenged the doctrine of the divine right of kings, which taught that the king was a law unto himself.

Instead, said Rutherford, the law (Lex) was king (Rex). The king and commoners alike were under the rule of law. Whose law? God's Law! In addition, English common law had developed from the foundation that man was accountable to a higher, fixed law ultimately based on God's Word, and was not free always to follow his own changing desires.[6] These ideas accounted for the comparatively peaceful and orderly revolution led by our founding fathers.

Mobilize People With the Same World View

At the same time, these ideas had a profound impact on England. It was in this context that John Wesley touched the heart of Great Britain. Historian Kenneth Scott Latourette observes that:

> The Wesleyan movement was not out to work basic changes in society. However, John Wesley persistently contended against such evils as bribery and corruption in politics, smuggling, and the plundering of wrecked vessels. Moreover, Wesley worked strenuously to relieve poverty and started missions to prisoners....Wesley, too, was a pioneer in the anti-slavery movement. He did much to mould the English middle class and to inculcate in it steadiness, sobriety, and industry, and to teach it to regard wealth as a trust.[7]

During Wesley's lifetime, through his biblically based ideas, England was dramatically changed for the better.

Vladimir Lenin understood the power of ideas. In 1903, in London, England, a group of several hundred people gathered for a meeting of the Russian Social Democratic Labor Party. Members of the party took seriously the writing and teaching of Karl Marx who, in the mid-1800s, had penned *The Communist Manifesto* and *Das Kapital*. During the convention, the question was raised concerning who should be considered eligible for membership in the party. Many believed it should be open to all who were willing to join. In the midst of the debate, Lenin jumped to his feet and argued vehemently that the only person worthy of being a Communist was a person who had died to everything else in life in order to dedicate the rest of his life to the cause. In the end, he was joined by a small band of seventeen followers. To them he said, "You are men of destiny. You can conquer the world."

Under Lenin's leadership, it took that small band of men just fourteen years to complete a revolution that captured all of Russia. At the time of the Bolshevik Revolution in 1917, there were only about four thousand members of the Communist Party. Just four thousand men and a powerful idea captured a country which at that time had a population of 150 million people![8]

There cannot be a revolution without ideas, for what we think about determines our actions. And what we think about most determines the course of our lives. One person with a powerful idea can influence millions. A few people acting on their ideas can change the course of history.

Madalyn Murray O'Hair believed so strongly that prayer did not belong in public schools that she personally pushed the case that led to the fateful Supreme Court decision of 1962. Her son writes, "The expenses of the paperwork and court fees involved in pursuing the appeal through the courts were not too high. In fact, as I recall, removing prayer from U.S. public schools cost less than $20,000."[9] Bill Murray also notes that "no Christian organization filed a brief in support of our opponents (Baltimore Board of Education)."[10]

Beverly LaHaye has mobilized 500,000 women since 1979.[11] This group, Concerned Women for America, has become a strong force to combat the onslaught of secular thinking that has attacked the traditional, biblically based view of the family.

Before you can do anything to help change our nation, you must know your world view. You may think that is easy, that it is already settled in your mind. *Be careful!* You may find that the reason you are not having a significant impact is that your world view generally agrees with the prevailing ideas of our society.

Summary

- You must have an idea worth fighting for.
- You can make a difference by realizing that ideas originate from a person's world view.
- You can make a difference by mobilizing enough people who hold the same biblical world view.

ACTION STEP

Ask yourself: Will I and my biblical world view make a difference in this world?

How? List three ways:

1. _____

2. _____

3. _____

4

THE BATTLE OF WORLD VIEWS

T hese are a few of the catchy phrases that reflect what many in our society believe:

"Do your own thing."
"Let's get physical."
"Just use common sense."
"Whatever will be, will be."
"You can't legislate morality."
"Don't be so narrow-minded."
"How could anything be wrong when it feels so right?"
"Look out for number one."

The world views represented by these phrases are often accepted without biblical evaluation by many Christians. They have been, as J. B. Phillips puts it, squeezed into the world's mold.[1] Satan seeks to have us think that these phrases are harmless. But as we use them, the assumptions underlying them subtly become ours and thereby dull our spiritual vitality and impact.

The fact is, your world view is a life and death issue. Why? Because ideas have consequences. Our world view either consciously or unconsciously shapes our ideas, thoughts, attitudes, beliefs and values. Ideas produce preferences and convictions which lead to action, or to inaction. That can have dramatic consequences.

Consider Arthur Koestler, a prominent author and philosopher who believed that man was the result of an "evolutionary blunder." His belief led him to the conclusion that life held no purpose. In March of 1983, the seventy-seven-year-old writer and his wife were found dead, the result of barbiturate overdoses, in an apparent suicide pact.

Futility of Atheism

Just before his death, Thomas Paine, a renowned political writer in the late 1700s, faced the full implications of his world view. During his final moments on earth, he said, "I would give worlds, if I had them, that *Age of Reason* had not been published....O God what have I done to suffer so much? But there is no God! But if there should be, what will become of me hereafter? Stay with me, for God's sake! Send even a child to stay with me, for it is hell to be alone. If ever the devil had an agent, I have been that one."[2]

Koestler and Paine reveal the futility of a world view that leaves God out of the picture. Yet theirs is the current prevailing world view in our society. It is called humanism. Humanism is not a scare word to frighten Christians. It does not mean humanitarianism or classical learning in this context. It is a well-defined world view, which its proponents call a religion without acknowledging a transcendent and immanent sovereign God.

Humanism Is a Religion

Spokesman Paul Kurtz defines humanism in his book *In Defense of Secular Humanism* as having three components: (1) an outlook on man based on science; (2) a method of inquiry that uses critical intelligence and rational inquiry to understand the world and solve problems, with resulting truth being the product of give and take among competing points of view; and (3) a set of moral values built within individuals and grounded in human experience.[3]

Secular humanism has a well-defined creed spelled out in two Manifestos. The first Manifesto in 1933 set forth fifteen tenets of "religious humanism" and con-. cluded:

> Though we consider the religious forms and ideas of our fathers no longer adequate, the quest for the good life is still the central task for mankind. Man is at last becoming aware that he alone is responsible for the realization of the world of his dreams, that he has within himself the power for its achievement. He must set intelligence and will to the task.[4]

The Supreme Court agreed that humanism is a religion in its 1961 decision in the case of *Torcaso v. Watkins*.[5] The second Manifesto, completed in 1973 and signed by 114 prominent individuals, clearly spelled out this religious philosophy:

- No deity will save us; we must save ourselves.
- Promises of immortal salvation or fear of eternal damnation are both illusory and harmful.
- ...moral values derive their source from human experience. Ethics is autonomous and situational, needing no theological or ideological sanction.
- Reason and intelligence are the most effective instruments that humankind possesses.
- ...commitment to all humankind is the highest commitment of which we are capable....Humanism thus interpreted is a moral force that has time on its side. We believe that humankind has the potential intelligence, good will, and cooperative skill to implement this commitment in the decades ahead.[6]

There are those who would say that the goals of humanism are laudable. We would agree that the religion of humanism is searching for the truth and that it is concerned about man and his destiny. Where we differ is in the belief that mankind can solve his problems using only his own intellect and ingenuity.

We believe that man cannot and will not succeed without an acknowledgment of a sovereign God actively controlling the universe. Advocates of humanism must ultimately admit that life has no meaning or that meaning must be personally defined, since it allows no transcendent values and denies the existence of the supernatural realm.

From Secular to Cosmic Humanism

Even so, we are already seeing the transition from purely secular humanism to cosmic humanism, bringing a spiritual dimension to the philosophy.

Cosmic humanism is a blending of humanist philosophy and eastern-occult mysticism in which man is striving to develop godlike capabilities. Swami Vivekananda states it most clearly: "The great central truth in every religion: to evolve a God out of man."[7]

Cosmic humanism is the philosophy that pervades what is often referred to as the New Age Movement. It has many forms of expression—holistic health,[8] confluent education, the human potential movement, transpersonal and self-actualization psychology, new consciousness, and many more phrases. According to Douglas Groothuis, author of *Unmasking the New Age*, the New Age Movement has six distinctive doctrines: (1) All is One; (2) All is God; (3) Humanity is God; (4) We are all in need of a changed consciousness; (5) All religions are one; (6) Cosmic evolutionary optimism will bring it all to pass.[9] Regardless of the means, the goal is similar: a new world order based on one religion and one economic system as the only means to provide peace and prosperity for all mankind.

When we come to the Christian and biblical world view, we must agree with John Oswalt when he says:

> It is sometimes implied that the biblical teachings are a vast hodgepodge of materials, somehow thrown together. That is not true. Once it is understood how the Bible sees the world and what a radical departure that view is from the pagan world view, many teachings that seem quaint and unrelated suddenly take their places as integral parts of a system that has powerful claims on the lives of people today.[10]

Humanism and Biblical Christianity in Conflict

Thus the conflict between a biblical world view and humanism, whether secular or cosmic, is inevitable. The

Christian world view differs radically from all other world views in that:

- It views God as the ultimate source of truth and authority.
- It views Jesus Christ as Lord of all areas of life.
- It views the Bible as God's special revelation and the final and sufficient authority for man.
- It views man as created by God, yet fallen and sinful, in need of God's redemption, through Jesus Christ alone.

It is impossible to view our world from a position of neutrality. Either the transcendent God is honored as the supreme sovereign, or He is not. Either God is acknowledged as the one true source of power, truth and good, or He is not. Either God and His Word are considered the source of ultimate authority, or they are not. Every human being has faith in something, and that faith affects his understanding and actions in every area of life.

We realize the kingdom of darkness has many manifestations other than our descriptions of secular and cosmic humanism. We also realize there are many systems for categorizing a world view position. But it all boils down to the very issue with which Satan confronted Eve in the Garden when he told her, "You will be like God!" Either God is supreme or man is supreme. Either God and His revealed Word are our ultimate standard for determining truth, good and evil, or man is. If it is man, we have no absolutes. All is relative, and every man can do what is right in his own eyes.

The apostle John, in his first letter, warned the early church of this same spirit, the spirit of antichrist. It is this spirit that is behind all world views other than the biblical one. John wrote: "And who is the greatest liar? The one who says that Jesus is not Christ. Such a person is antichrist, for he does not believe in God the Father and in His Son. For a person who doesn't believe in Christ, God's Son, can't have God the Father either. But he who has Christ, God's Son, has God the Father also" (1 John 2:22,23, The Living Bible). John has captured the essence of the conflict—Christ or antichrist! Christ is the ultimate standard for all men.

In this book we will focus our attention primarily on secular humanism because of its pervasive influence in Western culture today. Secular humanism is a current major threat of the spirit of antichrist.

The Impact of a Biblical World View

Sir William Blackstone, the esteemed professor of law at Oxford, produced what is still considered one of the most thorough treatments of English law ever produced by one man. His *Commentaries on the Laws of England*, published in the 1760s, became the standard of legal textbooks for students in England and the United States. He recognized that the fear of God was the beginning of wisdom, and therefore began his *Commentaries* with a careful analysis of the law of God as revealed in the Bible.

> The doctrines thus delivered we call the revealed or divine law, and they are to be found only in the Holy Scriptures. Upon these two foundations, the law of nature and the law of revelation, depend all human laws; that is to say, no human laws should be suffered to contradict these.[11]

For more than 150 years, Blackstone's biblical world view matched that of English and American society and their law schools. Today, however, Blackstone's *Commentaries*, once the basis of instruction in most law schools, are viewed as curiosities, to be dragged out only in a course on legal history.

Alexis de Tocqueville observed in his examination of the United States in the mid-1800s:

> America is still the place where the Christian religion has kept the greatest real power over men's souls and nothing better demonstrates how useful and natural it is to man, since the country where it now has the widest sway is both the most enlightened and the freest....[12]

In 1665, Hugo Grotius beautifully explained how societal rule begins with the rule of God in the individual. We would do well to remember his words today:

> He knows not how to rule a kingdome, that cannot manage

a Province; nor can he wield a Province, that cannot order a City; nor he a Village, that cannot guide a Family; nor can that man Govern well a Family that knows not how to Govern himselfe; neither can any Govern himselfe unless his reason be Lord, Will and Appetite her Vassals: nor can Reason rule unlesse herselfe be ruled by God, and (wholy) be obedient to Him.[13]

A Little Bit of Humanism in All of Us?

Now all of this discussion about cosmic and secular humanism as a world view may seem a bit academic and theoretical to you, but it applies in the most subtle and yet penetrating way. For instance, you would probably not call yourself a "humanist," but how do you really view life?

- Do you evaluate your time and resource utilization based on your own objectives or on the objectives of the Scriptures (living for eternity)?[14]
- Do you get most of your guidance on life from the Word of God and godly counsel or from "other" sources?[15]
- Does your Christian life consist of church and a Bible study or two or does it permeate every aspect of your life?[16]
- Do you work in order to have fun and recreate or do you recreate in order to have fulfillment in all of your work?[17]
- Have you chosen a career based on biblical conviction or have you simply patterned your life based on others' expectations?[18]

It is subtle, isn't it? Do you see how easy it is to get drawn into the world system? Most of us do not want it to happen. In fact, we are shocked to think that we are "worldly," but that is the plague of contemporary, orthodox Christianity. We have lost our saltiness and witness and, thereby, our impact. We have become like the world. Too often, you cannot tell a Christian from a non-Christian. And, tragically, that leaves us Christians serving Satan instead of God. Think of that! But we will never see this altered until we change our minds or repent of our thinking patterns and presuppositions. Nothing short of an all-out offensive to develop a biblical world and life view will work!

The problem is serious, but our thought patterns can be changed if we deliberately set out to think biblically and saturate our minds with the Word of God and biblical principles.

The place to start is to believe and act upon what we already know.

In 1983, the combined houses of Congress passed a resolution declaring 1983 the "Year of the Bible." In a dramatic ceremony before three thousand people gathered at the Presidential Prayer Breakfast in Washington, D.C., President Reagan signed the document making it the official law of the land. In his address to the group that morning, the President said that if we as a nation would obey the Ten Commandments and the Golden Rule, every problem we face in America would be solved.

At first that sounds like a simplistic statement. Can racial problems, drug addiction, divorce, pornography, the national debt—can all of these problems be solved by obeying the Ten Commandments and the Golden Rule? On careful reflection, one is forced to agree with the President's claim.

If we are going to change our society, we must establish a biblical world view, both individually and corporately. But before we can do that, we must understand one more truth. Our battle is not, ultimately, against humanism or any other philosophy. It is a far more deadly battle. In fact, it is a war. Unless we understand the nature of this warfare, we shall never be successful in our revolution.

Summary

- World views determine our thoughts and actions.
- Both secular and cosmic humanism have become increasingly influential in our society.
- Biblical Christianity has a unique perspective on life that is in opposition to humanistic thinking.
- Too often Christians have been unknowingly influ-

enced by humanistic thinking rather than biblical thinking.

ACTION STEP

Ask yourself: In what ways have my thinking and living been affected by humanism?

5

KINGDOMS AT WAR:

Seeing the Unseen

It's a scene repeated thousands of times daily. A businessman boards a plane, removes his coat and leans back in his seat for a moment of reprieve from the pressures of work. He pulls out the airline magazine from the seat pocket in front of him. As he leafs through the publication, he passes a full-color picture of a sensuous woman in a bathing suit. He flips back for a closer look.

The alluring woman, with a rich suntan, is reclining on a sun-drenched beach in front of a resort hotel. "When you're in Miami," she says, "here's where you'll find me."

Now, why does he want to find her? She's not suggesting a game of checkers. She's suggesting sex. Such advertisements, filled with sexual overtones and other kinds of subliminal seduction, pervade nearly every form of mass media. And the media experts know that catering to the sexual drive is one of the most potent forms of selling anything.

Why are such advertisements so dangerous? They usually bypass our rational minds and appeal subliminally to our emotions. They reflect a deeper, more dangerous battle that rages around us, unseen by our eyes, yet every bit as real. Unless we recognize that battle, we will

41

never succeed in seeing a moral and spiritual revolution in our country.

War

We are at war!

"War [is] a state of open, armed, often prolonged conflict carried on between nations, states, or parties."[1] The plight of mankind has, from time immemorial, been plagued by war, hot and cold; by conflict, provoked and unprovoked; and by enmity, overt and covert.

The first declaration of war is recorded in Genesis 3:15 following the fall of Adam and Eve. God addresses the serpent, the tempter, saying, "And I will put enmity between you and the woman, and between your seed and her seed; he shall bruise you on the head, and you shall bruise him on the heel."

The battle lines are drawn—God's kingdom of light, life and righteousness versus Satan's kingdom of darkness, death and wickedness.[2] Mistakenly, we think it is God versus Satan. But God is *not* a direct combatant. He alone is sovereign and has determined the outcome of the battle.

Instead, it is man who is the agent for the temporal advancement of either kingdom. Man is the focal point of the conflict. Both God and Satan desire man's allegiance; God, through the obedience of faith, and Satan, through the deceptive promises of power, pleasure, fortune, and fame.

All men belong to one or the other of these two kingdoms. Since the fall of Adam, all men upon physical birth are subject to Satan's kingdom of darkness.[3] Satan continues his rebellion against God by seeking to deceive, to blind minds, to accuse Christians before God, and to tempt them to sin. The kingdom of Satan exists to oppose God and His plan for the world.[4]

For anyone to be rescued from Satan's kingdom and to gain entrance into God's kingdom of light, he must experience a spiritual birth. This takes place when one places his faith in Jesus Christ as his Savior and Lord.

He passes from darkness to light and from death into eternal life. He is indwelt by God's Holy Spirit.[5]

Once we have become citizens of God's kingdom, we are admonished to don the whole armor of God so we can resist the enemy and can "use God's mighty weapons, not those made by men, to knock down the devil's strongholds. These weapons can break down every proud argument against God and every wall that can be built to keep men from finding Him. With these weapons I can capture rebels and bring them back to God, and change them into men whose hearts' desire is obedience to Christ," through His written Word.[6]

It is crucial that every person recognize to which kingdom he belongs. Our responsibility as Christians is to promote the advancement of the kingdom of God. Our Commander-in-Chief has commanded in Matthew 28:19,20: "Go, make disciples of all the nations!"

Playground or Battlefield?

Instead, we are caught up in the mentality that this world is a playground rather than a battleground. A. W. Tozer put it well when he contrasted the attitude of our forefathers with that of our contemporaries:

> In the early days, when Christianity exercised a dominant influence over American thinking, men conceived the world to be a battleground. Our fathers believed in sin and the devil and hell as constituting one force; and they believed in God and righteousness and heaven as the other. These were opposed to each other in the nature of them forever in deep, grave, irreconcilable hostility. Man, so our fathers held, had to choose sides; he could not be neutral. For him it must be life or death, heaven or hell, and if he chose to come out on God's side he could expect open war with God's enemies. The fight would be real and deadly and would last as long as life continued here below....The Christian soldier...never forgot what kind of world he lived in. It was a battleground, and many were the wounded and the slain.

Tozer goes on to the modern mindset:

> How different today: the fact remains the same but the interpretation has changed completely. Men think of the world, not as a battleground but as a playground. We are not here to

fight, we are here to frolic. We are not in a foreign land, we are at home. We are not getting ready to live, we are already living, and the best we can do is to rid ourselves of our inhibitions and our frustrations and live this life to the full.[7]

If we are not even aware of the war, there is the danger of committing treason: "violation of allegiance toward one's sovereign or country; especially, the betrayal of one's own country by waging war against it or by consciously and purposely acting to aid its enemies."[8] Now most Christians are not consciously committing treason against God's kingdom; they would not think of it. But they are helping the enemy, just the same.

Just as there were U.S. companies who sent raw materials to Japan prior to World War II, today there are U.S. companies sending valuable materials and technologies, such as computers and electronic components, to nations who wish to see the demise of the United States. Likewise, there are Christians who consciously or unconsciously subscribe to the philosophy of this world's humanistic system, and thereby contribute to the advancement of Satan's kingdom of darkness.

You might ask how this is possible. For example, have you ever plopped yourself into an easy chair to relax a bit and indiscriminately watched a few minutes of television? You might have rationalized this by saying to yourself, "I deserve a break today." But perhaps you failed to realize that in those few moments of mental neutrality the enemy might have shot one of his fiery darts into your mind. Maybe it was just a sexual innuendo or the Lord's name used to punctuate a sentence. In that unguarded moment, however, a seed may have been planted or watered that can contribute to the development of a non-biblical pattern of thinking in you—a mental pattern or world view that advances Satan's kingdom of darkness. And not only does that affect you, but through your life it can affect others as well. Think of it! You could be unwittingly leading others toward the kingdom of darkness.

Yes, we *are* at war! We need to ask ourselves the question: Are cold-heartedness, indifference, dishonesty, immorality, unbelief, lack of love, and failure to discipline and renew our minds advancing Satan's kingdom of darkness?

How are you doing in this battle of ideas? Are you winning the war of ideas, or are you being deceived and capitulating to the crafty wiles of Satan?

Which Side Are You On?

A committed, full-time Christian leader recently did some serious evaluation of his own warfare to see how he was doing in the battle of ideas. The outcome shocked and overwhelmed him. He found secular and humanistic thoughts creeping into his thinking in numerous areas. He was unknowingly being "conformed to the world" and succumbing to the "kingdom of darkness."[9] For instance, he found more fulfillment in position and power than in devotion to Christ.[10] Activity was winning over worship of Christ.[11] He was focusing more on pleasing people than on pleasing God.[12] He found himself toning down his messages and biblical convictions so as not to offend.[13] Natural skills were becoming the way to solve problems—not prayer, biblical wisdom, godly counsel and dependence on God.[14] Joy became conditioned by circumstances.[15] Personal attacks were being felt deeply and impeding his work. Stress was being internalized and causing times of anger and depression.[16]

"So what?" you say. "All of this is only *natural*. Any normal person would act like that, wouldn't he?"

Indeed, a *natural* person who was *normal* would act like that. And the lie of Satan is that we Christians are natural and normal. We are not! God has gifted us with His supernatural power, through the Holy Spirit, and we are His redeemed people, called out for a special purpose.[17] We are not perfect, but we are to live in the realm of God's supernatural power with a disciplined life-style obedient to Christ's Lordship. We should not be duped into thinking that we should live according to the prevailing patterns of society.

If we live as the world lives, we lose the battle of ideas and fall into the kingdom of darkness.

Bill was once asked to speak with a famous general in the United States military. The general said he believed in Christ and that He had died for his sins. He said he wanted to receive Christ, but something—he did not know what—held him back. After more than an hour, Bill opened his Bible to Colossians 1:13,14 and asked the man to read it aloud: "[God] has rescued us out of the darkness and gloom of Satan's kingdom and brought us into the kingdom of his dear Son, who bought our freedom with his blood and forgave us all our sins" (TLB).

The general had never realized that there were two kingdoms. "Which kingdom are you in?" Bill asked.

"I guess I'm in Satan's kingdom," the general answered.

"Do you want to remain a member of Satan's kingdom?" Bill asked.

"No."

"Then let me help liberate you. You do it by acknowledging that Jesus Christ is God and the Sovereign Ruler of the universe. He has liberated you by paying the penalty for your sins. You simply have to believe and pray, 'Lord Jesus, come into my heart, forgive my sins, liberate me from Satan's kingdom and make me a member of Your kingdom.'"

The general responded positively and with a sincere

prayer enlisted in God's kingdom. Immediately, his life-style began to change, and he became a vocal witness for biblical values, based on his new relationship with Jesus Christ.

Act Like a Citizen of the King

After you enter this kingdom, as you can right now through a prayer like the one above, you need to recognize that your new citizenship in Christ's kingdom of light makes you a citizen of heaven.[18] There are four ways we can act like a citizen of the King.

1. We must know who is our sovereign ruler.

God the Father through His Son Jesus Christ is the ruler of the kingdom of God. Satan is ruler of all those who have not submitted to the rule of God in their lives, no matter how moral, ethical and even religious they may be. No other choices exist.

Let's take another look at that hypothetical businessman we met at the beginning of this chapter. Is he serving God or Satan if he exaggerates on his resume, assuming his employer will never check the facts? Is he serving God or Satan if he stretches the truth in his advertising in order to attract more customers? Is he serving God or Satan if he uses his wealth to buy a vacation condominium, an extra sports car or a luxury motor boat, while giving little or nothing to the cause of Christ? Is he serving God or Satan if he attends church but does not seek to bring his commitment to Christ to his profession or sphere of influence? As long as a person does not have Jesus Christ as Lord, Satan is satisfied for the time being, for that person is contributing toward Satan's goal.

One may think he belongs to God's kingdom because he is a religious person. But if he is not in submission to God, he is, either knowingly or unknowingly, acting as an agent of Satan. The apostle John writes, "And how can we be sure that we belong to him? By looking within ourselves: are we really trying to do what he wants us to? Someone may say, 'I am a Christian; I am on my way to heaven; I belong to Christ.' But, if he doesn't do what

Christ tells him to, he is a liar."[19]

Satan will use any agency to further his plans, even the church. Certainly one can claim to believe in God, but unless his beliefs result in biblical actions he is promoting the kingdom of Satan. Those secular humanists and others who claim there is no God, who believe that man is ultimately master of his own destiny, are fulfilling the agenda of Satan and his kingdom. Those who adopt the cosmic humanist philosophy, though they embrace the spiritual and supernatural realm, still leave man as master of his own destiny, paying homage to a "force" that is actually Satan's.

Who is this ruler of the kingdom of darkness? He would like us to think of him as a funny-looking red creature. In reality he is one of the most beautiful beings God ever created. His original name was Lucifer,[20] and he was created by God and placed over all of the heavenly hosts. But, Lucifer was not content with his position, and he determined to become like God Himself. He led a revolt and took one third of the angels with him.[21] That revolt continues today, though it is hopeless, for God has made all the provisions for total victory.

Distinguished preacher and theologian Dr. Donald Gray Barnhouse explained:

> The evidence of Scripture and history shows that God chose...to give the rebel a full opportunity of exploiting every avenue of his power and wisdom so that it might be demonstrated that nothing good could ever come to the creation apart from that which originates in God Himself.[22]

2. To be effective citizens we need to understand the objective of our ruler.

God's desire is that all should come to know and experience Himself in the person of Jesus Christ. Only in this way can we fulfill the reason for which we were created—to have fellowship with God and, thus, bring glory to Him. In return, Jesus Christ gives us an abundant, joyful, eternal life. You need to know that God has a purpose for you.[23] In fact, you have an eternal destiny. Think of that! A destiny. If you don't fulfill your God-given destiny, nobody will. You are the only you there is. You

have a unique personality, gifts, relationships and resources. No one can copy or reproduce you.

So understand your purpose on this earth and seek
it with a passion.[24] We shall speak to this further in chapter 9.

According to Dr. Barnhouse, Satan's objective in the
battle of the Garden of Eden was twofold: "He wished to
detach man from God, and to attach man to himself. Man
is dependent upon God and if that dependence is destroyed, something must take its place; the devil hoped
that it would be a dependence upon himself."[25] Satan's
objectives are the same today. Secular humanism is his
shining success in the first objective. Cosmic humanism
is a movement toward the second goal.

**3. As citizens we need to understand and act
upon the provisions and privileges of our citizenship**.

The citizen of the kingdom of darkness demands his
rights. He insists on establishing his own rules and
guidelines. He considers himself master of his own fate,
responsible to no one but himself. Such a person eventually discovers that by claiming his "rights," in violation
of God's standards, he loses all real freedom. He makes
the same mistake as Satan, who sought to elevate himself
to equality with God only to lose all of his rights,
privileges and authority in heaven.[26]

The citizen of God's kingdom understands that he
has been purchased by God, as the apostle Paul explains:
"I have been crucified with Christ: and I myself no longer
live, but Christ lives in me. And the life I now have within
this body is a result of my trusting in the Son of God,
who loved me and gave himself for me."[27]

Jesus Christ said, "Seek first His kingdom, and His
righteousness."[28] Those who seek God's kingdom experience true joy and freedom. When you examine the characters of the Bible, you find that whenever people obeyed
God, they were joyful. When they disobeyed God, they
were miserable. That is one of the benefits of being a
citizen of God's kingdom—the promise of an abundant
life.[29]

In fact, it is the most exciting life imaginable. God calls His citizens ambassadors while they are on earth.[30] Once on an airplane, Ron was asked by the person sitting next to him what he did for a living. "I am an ambassador," Ron answered.

"You're a what?" asked the man seated next to Ron.

"I'm an ambassador," Ron said.

"What country do you represent?"

"Oh, I represent something far larger than a country."

"Do you represent a region or a continent?"

"Far greater than a region or a continent."

"What do you represent?"

"I represent a kingdom."

"What kind of kingdom?"

"The biggest! Wherever I go, I represent the King and His kingdom. I'm an ambassador of Jesus Christ." Ron went on to tell an interested man about Jesus Christ.

Eventually, everyone must acknowledge that God determines our destiny. We are either God's friend or His enemy. There is no option for neutrality or indifference. Jean-Paul Sartre, the famous French existentialist and humanistic philosopher, shortly before his death reversed his well-known views when he said, "I do not feel that I am the product of chance, a speck of dust in the universe, but someone who was expected, prepared, prefigured. In short, a being whom only a Creator could put here; and this idea of a creating hand refers to God."[31] Sartre had spent his life proclaiming there is no God, only to acknowledge Him at the end of his life.

4. As citizens we must understand the strategy of our ruler.

God's plans are clearly defined in Scripture, and we will spend much of the remainder of these pages examining those plans. But Satan's strategy is to divert our attention from God. He often does this subtly, in conflicts between husbands and wives and between parents and children. He does it by creating dissension in churches. He does it through employees who steal from their employers, even in such subtle ways as using their work phones for long distance calls of a personal nature. He does it by dulling Christians to the things that *penetrate* the *heart* of God—personal sin,[32] and societal sins such as pornography, abortion, racism, fraud, materialism, apathy, and others.

On a broader scale, Satan realizes the power of ideas and uses education, the mass media, advertising, and government as some of his tools for conveying his ideas to the masses. Systematically, he undermines rightful authority and moral values. He is the mastermind behind the advertisements that tell us in one way or another that we "only go around once in life," so we should grab for all the pleasure we can. Most of his subjects do not even know that they are his agents, which is another reason they are often so devastatingly effective.

We are involved in war, whether we choose to face it or not.

Martin Luther understood that fact when he said, "If I profess with the loudest voice and clearest exposition every portion of the truth of God except precisely that little point which the world and the devil are at the moment attacking, I am not confessing Christ, however boldly I may be professing Christ. Where the battle rages, there the loyalty of the soldier is proved and to be steady on all the battle front besides, is mere flight and disgrace if he flinches at that point."[33]

Since we are involved in a war, we cannot be silent or apathetic—we must speak out. As St. Ambrose wrote, "Not only for every idle word must man render an account, but also for every idle silence."[34] Or to put the same thought in the vernacular of today, "Silence is not always golden, sometimes it is just plain 'yellow.'"

Test Your Options

So, what options do we have? We can choose to ignore the warfare, but in doing so we are subtly supporting Satan. We can choose to support actively Satan's agenda through the philosophies of humanism. Or, we can choose to be part of God's kingdom and enlist in His army.

If we are actively involved in seeking God's kingdom and righteousness here on earth, there are several things we must realize. First, we must understand our sovereign's general strategy. Second, we must be trained in a few basics. Third, we must understand the basic characteristics of His subjects. Finally, we must be involved on one of the various fronts where the battle is raging. The rest of this book will examine each aspect of this war and the steps we can take to insure that we are on the winning side—His side.

Summary

- There are two kingdoms: Jesus Christ's kingdom of light and Satan's kingdom of darkness.
- You must know who is your sovereign ruler.
- You need to know the objectives of your ruler.
- You need to understand and act on the provisions and privileges of your citizenship.
- You must understand the strategy of your ruler.

ACTION STEP

Ask yourself: Of which kingdom am I a citizen? How do I know?

_____

_____

Do you act like a citizen of God's kingdom or of Satan's kingdom in your:

Family? _____

Business or work?_____

Use of money? _____

Leisure? _____

Your thought life? _____

Ministry? _____

Your conversation? _____

6

WAR STRATEGY:

We Need A Battle Plan

Who would threaten a lawsuit against the school board of Osseo, Minnesota, if they didn't stop the school choir from singing in churches at Christmas?[1] Who would file suit in federal court to have a Jewish menorrah and three crosses taken down in a public park?[2] Who has challenged an Arkansas state law requiring balanced treatment for the theories of evolution and creation? Who claims to be a defender of civil liberties in

'SILENT NIGHT' — BY THE CHILDREN OF THE FIFTH GRADE. ACCOMPANIST — MISS KELTMEN • ARRANGEMENT — ACLU

America? It is the American Civil Liberties Union (ACLU).

The American Civil Liberties Union is a highly influential organization in the United States. The founder, Roger Baldwin, was very clear about the organization's goals: He wanted to cause a working-class revolution within this country. Baldwin said:

> "... All my associates in the struggle for civil liberties take a class position, though many don't know it.... It is anti-capitalist and pro- revolutionary.... *The class struggle* is the central conflict of the world; all others are incidental."[3]

Undermining Judeo-Christian Values

Baldwin clearly knew where he was going! He had an aim. And the ACLU has been able to affect national policy through the court system. In the process, they have led the way in significantly undermining the influence of Judeo-Christian values in the American public arena.

They employ a strategy of intimidation designed to gain maximum results. They use the threat of legal action to force the cessation of any activity they consider undesirable. Some school boards and local governments don't have the resources to fight long, legal battles. When challenged by the ACLU, they will sometimes back down.

Conversely, when Christians have the opportunity to engage legal counsel to fight the ACLU, very often they expect "free representation" because of the perceived righteousness of their cause. Christians must "put their money where their mouth is" to meet the challenge. If the result of a direct confrontation was to prohibit school choirs from singing in local churches, or to delete "Silent Night" from kindergarten Christmas pageants, was it partly because Christians in their communities failed to back their concerns with finances?

The ACLU carefully picks its cases to gain decisions that will effectively change the law. They have led the way in cases that led to Supreme Court rulings in their favor in areas such as prayer in schools and abortion. They look for judges that favor their policies and lobby for their appointment to strategic positions on the bench. They cultivate working relationships with churches and organizations that support their objectives. They publicly label their opponents in ways that imply that they are outside the American mainstream.

The point is that they use effective, widely-practiced strategies and tactics. Their efforts have been most effective and as a result, many religious freedoms in the public arena have been lost through their interpretation of the phrase "separation of church and state." Much as many people deplore many of the things that they've done, we can learn from their use of strategy and seek to actively counter that part of their work with which we disagree.

The Principles of War: Understand the Objective

How do we win a war? We need a strategy that follows some basic principles. There are a few essential ingredients required for one kingdom to defeat another. James I. Wilson listed ten such requirements in a little book titled *The Principles of War.*[4] Understanding those principles, which we have used as the outline for this chapter, provides a good foundation if we are to be successful in our effort to win the war of ideas.

The apostle Paul wrote that we are to run the race, not for the pleasure of participating, but to *win.*[5] God has placed us on earth with a Great Commission, to take the gospel to all people throughout the world and to make disciples of all nations.[6] *That* is our objective, not just building churches or being happy with doing good. Too often Christians cannot be distinguished from non-Christians who happen to practice good morals. This is part of Satan's strategy to neutralize us. We must daily and deliberately refocus our goal to *help change lives.* We are to win people to Christ and help them become obedient to *all* that God has commanded.[7]

Have you ever asked yourself why you do what you do; why you have your particular job; why you spend your time and money as you do; why you belong to various clubs; even why you go to church? Is it because these things fulfill your God-given objectives or is it out of habit, impulse or because of what others do?

Offensive Strategy: Have a Plan

Baron Henri Jomini, a 19th century Swiss general, wrote, "They want war too methodical, too measured; I would make it brisk, bold, impetuous, perhaps sometimes even audacious."

We are told in Scripture to plan and to count the cost.[8] However, even though deliberation is vital, too often we analyze and strategize to the point where we are paralyzed. We need to take bold, aggressive action. We need to "redeem the time" and "buy up the opportunity" as Paul tells us in Ephesians 5:15,16 and Colossians 4:5. This is done as we respond to the Spirit of God's direction consistent with God's Word and move aggressively to take the initiative. We must be able to react when the need is there.

One man in a northern California city had a bold offensive plan. He contacted the ten most influential leaders in the community and asked each of them to meet four times with the other nine. They included the senior judge, owner of the local newspaper, chairman of the board of supervisors, president of Rotary, and manager of the largest bank.

The meetings followed no specific agenda. The purpose was for community leaders to meet together, talk, and become friends. Though many were not Christians, they prayed, looked into the Gospel of John, and discussed the implication of the Bible in their lives. Those same ten men continued to meet weekly for the next several years, and at least fifteen other similar groups sprouted up throughout the city. Many came to Christ through the friendly interaction, but those who did not still felt comfortable with the group.

One man, a leader in his county's political affairs, when approached about joining a group said, "Men, you don't know how much I need this. There's a little Episcopal church that stays open twenty-four hours a day. Sometimes, after our meetings, I'll go there and sit for half an hour and think, just trying to get some clarity into the decisions I have to make. I really need a group like this."

Other times, family struggles, including surgery, divorce and children on drugs, have been shared. The friendships that have been developed have given the security and freedom to share and care for each other.

Concentration: Focus Our Efforts

Battles are won when we concentrate our efforts rather than go in too many directions at once. We need men and women to help in the battle against poverty, to minister in the ghettos, skid rows and prisons.

But if we are going to effectively change our nation, we must also target our efforts on present and future leaders, men and women of influence who in turn will bring others with them.

Though each person needs to concentrate his ministry on the area to which God leads him, we suggest that those in positions of leadership start to develop clear strategies to build new leaders as well as challenge existing leaders in their current sphere of influence. Changed institutions help produce changed societies. And changed leaders help produce changed institutions, which in turn change society. We must concentrate, therefore, on winning current and potential leaders to Christ and seeing them develop into committed Christians. Their influence will achieve great gains in reclaiming our culture for Christ.

In order for this obedience to be developed in an individual and, ultimately, a society, we must clearly remember the *vital* nature of the mind. For we are to be "transformed by the renewing of the mind."[9]

We can also learn much from the strategies of guerrilla warfare, which is prevalent today. (See Appendixes B and C.) Indeed, much of our spiritual battle is closely related to this type of warfare as well as to conventional warfare, for guerrilla warfare focuses on the mind, thoughts and ideology. Its objective is, first, *to win the minds of men.*

Two students of this form of battle have said:

> As a form of war, guerrilla warfare consists of imposing one's own will on an opponent, and thus destroying the opponent's will and strength to resist. In its simplest form, guerrilla warfare aims at the conquest of the enemy. But to accomplish this, the guerrillas, unlike regular armies, emphasize attacking the determination and the mind of the opponent first, and his armies next.[10]

In guerrilla warfare, *the mind is attacked through an ideological appeal.*

> Basically, it is an ideological appeal, carefully tuned to justice, honour, pride and emotion. Its final goal is the capture of the human mind so that the people will participate in a violent struggle. Guerrilla leaders know well that human beings are slaves to their minds. Consequently, once the cause has its grip on the people's mind, they cannot but comply.[11]

Charles Thayer, a student of guerrilla warfare, has stated that three elements are critical to this thrust:

1. The cause must be both plausible and compelling.
2. It must possess a high moral appeal that justifies violations of traditional norms of behavior.
3. It has some hope of fulfillment.[12]

While we reject the "end justifies the means" tone of the second statement and the general revolutionary and destructive philosophy these statements might represent, these three elements demonstrate the need to present a biblical view of the world and life which is compelling, morally appealing and has a positive hope for the future, for the individual and for society.

We, as Christians, must recapture the initiative and strategy in winning the battle for the minds of men. We are not seeking to impose any human viewpoint, but rather we are exposing men to the mind and will of Jesus Christ.

In the two major passages of Scripture that deal with spiritual warfare, Ephesians 6:10-18 and 2 Corinthians 10:3-6, we read of the absolute necessity of this kind of spiritual war for the mind. In Ephesians 6, we are to protect our minds and do battle with ideologies with the "sword of the Spirit which is the Word of God." In 2 Corinthians 10, we are to "bring down fortresses" (world views, presuppositions, assumptions, philosophies, feelings and opinions) that are contrary to the Word of God.

Mobilization: Moving Your Resources Quickly

In war, you must be able to move your resources quickly. The apostle Paul was mobile and strategically sound in his efforts, and the result was that all Asia Minor heard the gospel. We must learn to respond to the need with our resources. For instance, those in local businesses should use their influence to mobilize people and resources to counter secular attacks. One female executive in Palm Springs stopped the Playboy channel from coming to the local cable system by organizing a write-in campaign. When she called the station manager to ask why he stopped this channel from coming over the cable system, he said it was because of all the mail and calls he had received against it. *Mobilization works!*

Security: Know Your Enemy

Security involves having quality intelligence about your enemy and providing continual protection against the enemy, and it means having a final line of defense past which the enemy cannot penetrate. The famous Prussian General Karl von Clausewitz wrote in his treatise, *Principles of War,* "The art of retrenchment...shall serve the defender not to defend himself more securely behind the rampart, but to attack the enemy more successfully."[13]

Knowing the enemy is crucial to our success. We need to study Satan's tactics. We need to remember that he can masquerade as an "angel of light." He is attractive, subtle and winsome. He will attack at our most vulnerable spots. He will delude. He will seek to dull us to the things of Christ and direct us into a subtle conformity to the world system.

We need to study the strategies of secular and cosmic humanists, cultists, and false religionists. Satan is wise, and we can learn from observing his tactics.

Ron sat in a doctoral class in the education department at Harvard and heard a lawyer who was also a professor at the Maharishi Academy of Natural Law in Cambridge, Massachusetts. The Academy is an extension of the Maharishi University in Fairfield, Iowa. From a human perspective he gave a brilliant, convincing lecture on how Transcendental Meditation was the ultimate key to finding peace in life. These disciples of Maharishi Mahesh Yogi, who advocate many of the tenets of cosmic humanism including Transcendental Meditation (TM), are trying to penetrate the top thinkers of America and win them to their point of view. Why are we not doing the same?

Also, knowledge of the opposition's operations is essential. Using our guerrilla warfare analogy:

> The guerrillas, who cannot fight except on their own terms, must know enough about their enemy's plans and movements to avoid being trapped into battles which they cannot win; they must have sufficient knowledge of the enemy's weaknesses to make their own strikes as safe and effective as possible.[14]

But where do we get such information? That is easy; first, we go to Scripture to know the genuine truth so well that we can recognize the counterfeits of Satan's kingdom. We need to study the tactics of our real enemy, Satan, so that we are not "ignorant of his schemes."[15] Second, we need to read, with discernment, the magazines, books and newspapers that promote non-biblical values. We further need to watch and listen to the media that influence the minds of people, and talk to people wherever we go to understand their thinking. Third, leaders and pastors, who are limited by time and resources, should constantly seek the counsel of specialists who research and evaluate the ideologies and strategies of men who are the agents of our enemy, Satan. We need to find, observe, and listen to reliable counsel to raise our sensitivities to what is going on around us, so that we know how best to respond to the attacks that arise.

Dr. Glenn Olds, president of Alaska Pacific University and past president of Kent State University, reported that, in the intense investigation that followed the death of four students when National Guard troops marched on campus to break up a demonstration, they discovered that none of the leaders was a student. They were Communists strategically placed on campus to organize the entire student body. Although Communists used this strategy for evil, we can use it for good.

Surprise: Do Not Broadcast Your Plans

Satan is a master of surprise, and often he does it by slowly desensitizing us, lulling us to sleep so that we are unaware of his schemes. By contrast, too often Christians broadcast all they do. Perhaps we sense a need to have the spotlight, or perhaps we are just naive. There are times we need to keep quiet. Dr. Steven F. Hotze learned this in Houston. In an attempt to defeat proposed legislation favorable to homosexuals, he organized a low-profile, grass roots campaign. When the news finally reached the media, it was too late. The homosexual rights ordinance was overturned by an 81 to 19 percent margin.

We might also start various "front" groups. One of the most effective Christian movements in the late '60s and early '70s was the Christian World Liberation Front at the University of California, Berkeley. It was organized to counteract the radical movement on campus. Few people knew that its leaders were on the staff of Campus Crusade for Christ. They adopted the appearance and some of the methods of the radical left, and were so successful that eventually there was more talk on campus about Jesus Christ than about Karl Marx. Many believed it helped to defuse the radical leftist movement on that campus and helped to launch the Jesus Movement.

Christians are to be honest and direct.[16] However, we are to be prudent, cautious and "wise as serpents."[17]

Cooperation: We Must Work Together

We will be most effective if everyone works together as a team. Perhaps this is one area where Satan has accomplished most, by keeping Christians from working together. Jesus, in His prayer the night before His crucifixion, said, "My prayer for all of them is that they will be of one heart and mind, just as you and I are, Father."[18]

The point is clear: We Christians must realize that we are allies, not opponents. We must submit ourselves to one army and one commander—Jesus Christ. We must be willing to cooperate and share resources, realizing our various gifts and talents, so that we can maximize our influence for Christ and His kingdom.

Communication: The Vital Link

The official definition of communication is "All the routes, land, water and air, which connect an operating military force with its base of operations, along which supplies and reinforcements move."[19] Many wars have been lost because people have over-extended their lines of supply, and contact with their troops has been lost. If we are going to win our battles against Satan, we must learn to communicate effectively with one another. We must keep in touch. And we must begin only those offensive actions for which we can provide resources on a consistent basis to see our strategies through to victory.

There are signs that Christian leaders are opening those lines of communication. We need to continue that effort. Key leaders must network. In every city there ought to be a group of spiritual leaders like the "Salt Shakers" in Portland, Oregon, who meet to mobilize for the sake of righteousness in the city. Men of different theological bents meet to cooperate on common concerns in the same way committed lawyers, executives, and others need to network nationally in order to share ideas and mobilize resources.

We do not need more massive ecumenical organizations. We do not need to compromise or water down our own programs or beliefs to work together. In fact, that often inhibits impact because it neutralizes distinctives and convictions.

However, coming together to strategize over common concerns can become a powerful tool in resource maximization.

For example, consider the Year of the Bible. Legislation calling upon President Reagan to proclaim 1983 the Year of the Bible in the United States was passed by both houses of Congress and signed by the President, who subsequently issued the requested proclamation. In connection with these actions, Bill formed and chaired a national committee to make the country as a whole aware of the Year of the Bible observance and to serve as a catalyst for maximum citizen involvement in it. Ron served as an executive committee member of this nonprofit, nongovernmental, volunteer group, of which the President agreed to serve as honorary chairman.

We saw God do miraculous things as Protestants, Roman Catholics, Eastern Orthodox and Jews came together around common concerns. No one compromised his or her convictions, but each stimulated the others to elevate the Word of God in this land.

In view of the interfaith nature of the National Committee for the Year of the Bible, evangelism was, of course, not one of the group's activities. At the same time, individual Americans and organizations were naturally at liberty to relate to the Year of the Bible observance as they felt appropriate.

In one dramatic case, for instance, the Year of the Bible stimulated Mrs. Arthur S. De Moss, another executive committee member, to develop and implement, through her family's charitable foundation, a plan to make the Bible and Jesus Christ an attractive "option" in our country. Her efforts led to a tasteful, biblically oriented public information effort that was the most successful in media history in terms of response. More than eleven million Americans throughout the nation telephoned or wrote to request the *Power for Living* book mentioned in the foundation's thought-provoking advertisements in magazines and on television. The book, which was offered free of charge, presented the claims of Christ in an accurate and attractive manner.

Subsequently, inspired by the unprecedented success of the *Power for Living* effort, Christian Broadcasting Network president Dr. Pat Robertson sponsored a most successful campaign to promote *The Book* (an edition of *The Living Bible*). His effort resulted in the distribution of many millions of copies of the Scriptures.

Economy: Maximize Your Resources

General Karl Von Clausewitz wrote, "The more the concentration can be compressed into one act and one moment, the more perfect are its results."[20] This principle was used in Gideon's victory over the armies of Midian as described in Judges 7 and 8. Under God's direction, Gideon sent home 31,700 men and won the battle with three hundred men.[21]

Sometimes we are more effective with a small number of strategically well-equipped people than with a large number of people who are ill-equipped. We can look to the examples of John Wesley and George Whitefield who influenced England, and to Wilberforce, who, from his position in Parliament, did much to change the social climate of the nation.

Recently, an Atlanta executive, Jerry Nims, employed this principle when he mobilized a number of influential persons in Atlanta to counter homosexuality. His insight and action caused a reversal in a trend in that city. When the press sought to attack his position as bigoted, his well-thought-through explanation of his concern—calling homosexuality "militant moral anarchy"—dramatically changed the tenor of the newspaper articles and the battle in the city. He took the offensive by seizing the moral high ground and his effort was successful.

Pursuit: The Battle Is Not Over

We need to realize that we have victory over Satan. The battle is already won. He cannot withstand the power of the Body of Christ. But we need to pursue the already beaten enemy. Once Gideon broke through the Midian army with his three hundred men, he called for the men he had sent home, and they helped him in the mop-up operation. Though Gideon had already won the battle, he did not stop his pursuit until the enemy was totally destroyed.

Christians have a tendency to enjoy a partial victory and then relax. We need tenacious, persevering, aggressive action. We must not relax our efforts, for the enemy never stops. Satan and his demons are like defeated soldiers who head to the hills and continue to conduct guerrilla warfare. We must remember the words of Winston Churchill, who in the dark days of 1941 spoke these great words at Harrow School:

> For everyone, surely, what we have gone through in this period...this is the lesson: never give in, never give in, *never, never, never, never*—in nothing, great or small, large or petty— never give in except to convictions of honour and good sense. Never yield to force; never yield to the apparently overwhelming might of the enemy.[22]

Though each person must apply these principles to his own personal warfare and ministry, we suggest the need for a more wholistic strategy built on making an impact on our society at several levels and on numerous fronts.

Ron remembers walking into the Aspen Institute of Humanistic Studies in Aspen, Colorado, a few years ago and sitting in on a meeting with sixty of the leading opinion influencers in America who were strategizing on how to permeate our society with a humanistic perspective. Since that time, he has uncovered some very fine research on the various strategies of this entity. Their strategies are sophisticated and well thought through. But their goals are definitely not Christian.

Similarly, the followers of Sun Myung Moon (whose writings indicate he sees himself as the new Messiah) have a strategy; militant Islam has a strategy; the Communists have a strategy; the homosexual movement has a strategy; indeed, most movements have a strategy. But, as a general practice, we Christians tend to find ourselves with no plan, divided, defeated and discouraged.

It is time we brought together the best thinkers, strategists, tacticians and overall leaders from the Body of Christ to develop a wholistic, calculated strategy to reach our objectives, to fulfill the Great Commission and penetrate our society. Our strategies need to be comprehensive, yet targeted and deliberate. We should wait no longer to get back into the battle.

Summary

- Satan's agents usually seem to have very well-defined objectives, targets and strategies.
- Principles of conventional warfare and guerrilla warfare give us good insight into the battle between the kingdom of darkness and kingdom of light.
- The battle for the minds of men is the primary arena of this war.
- Christians need to start thinking strategically about the battle for the minds and lives of men.

ACTION STEP

What is your strategy for taking captive your sphere of influence "to the obedience of Christ"? Take a moment to determine how you can apply each of these principles to reach your sphere of influence for Christ (in your neighborhood, business, the local media, and other arenas where you live and work).

Principle 1: Understand the objective: What are your objectives?

_____

_____

Principle 2: An offensive strategy: What is your strategy?

_____

_____

Principle 3: The principle of concentration: Where will you concentrate your time and resources?

Principle 4: The principle of mobilization: How can you mobilize others to move quickly to respond to a problem?

Principle 5: The principle of security: After reading this book, examine our Recommended Resource list. List two newsletters or magazines you will subscribe to in order to know what the enemy is doing.

Principle 6: The principle of surprise: Will you commit yourself to wisely keeping what you and others are doing appropriately confidential?

Principle 7: The principle of cooperation: List individuals and perhaps organizations you will work with to achieve your objectives.

Principle 8: The principle of communication: Will you commit yourself to keeping current in communicating with others with whom you work in the battle?

_____

_____

Principle 9: The economy of force: List your resources:

_____

_____

Principle 10: The principle of pursuit: Will you commit yourself to not giving up when the battle becomes hard and you become tired?

_____

_____

7

THINK BIBLICALLY:

The Strategic Command Center

T he late Martin Neimoller painted a stark picture of what happened in Germany with the rise of Hitler and the subsequent holocaust in which more than eleven million people (Jews, Gypsies, aged, mentally ill) were exterminated:

In Germany
they first came for the Communists
and I didn't speak up because I wasn't a Communist.
Then they came for the Jews,
and I didn't speak up because I wasn't a Jew.
Then they came for the Trade Unionists,
and I didn't speak up because I wasn't a Trade Unionist.
Then they came for the Catholics,
and I didn't speak up because I was a Protestant.
Then they came for me...and by that time
there was no one left to speak up.[1]

Most of us, when we think of that time, are justifiably appalled and perhaps a bit judgmental. Few of us think about what we might have done to prevent it. There were millions of Christians attending church every Sunday in Germany during the 1930s, but with only a few exceptions, they did nothing to prevent their nation's humiliation. In fact, many justified it and supported their government's policies.

We would argue that an even greater holocaust is taking place in America today with the slaughter of one-and-a-half million babies each year through abortion. In the past twenty-five years, there has been a dramatic deterioration of traditional values and moral fiber of this nation. But how do we know when to react? On what basis do we act? How does one develop a response that is consistent with his confession as a Christian?

We do it by learning to challenge the world's views with God's views. We begin by acknowledging that all things are made by God, for God. The apostle Paul wrote, "In Him all things were created, both in the heavens and on earth, visible and invisible...all things have been created through Him and for Him."[2]

The Awesome Power of the Mind

In order to have any significant impact on society, Christians must learn to think and act biblically. We must learn to consistently think God's thoughts and bring them to bear on all situations. It must become a habit because our minds and thinking are the battlefield. Someone has well said:

Sow a thought, reap an act;
Sow an act, reap a habit;
Sow a habit, reap a character;
Sow a character, reap a destiny.

The point is that our thoughts greatly influence who we are and what we will become. This is why the Bible clearly says we are to be "transformed by the renewing of our minds."[3]

Think ... Think ... Think Biblically!

That means we must learn to evaluate an issue or situation by applying the truths and principles of Scripture. What does God's Word say about this matter? Each of us, like a builder, needs tools—such as a tape measure, square, and plumbline—to assure accuracy in what we build. C.S. Lewis, in *Mere Christianity*, says, "A man does not call a line crooked unless he has some idea of a straight line."[4] Without an objective, absolute, trustworthy standard, there can be no assurance of truth. Without God's special revelation, man is adrift on the sea of humanistic speculation and relativism. There can be no sense of confidence and certainty.

God has not left us without an absolute standard. He has given us His Word—the Bible—as "The Manufacturer's Handbook of Life and Living." First, it tells us about God—who He is. Second, it reveals the true origin, nature, and fall of man, as a created being who is to reflect God's image and likeness. Third, it tells us about the created world in which we have been placed as vice-regents to rule as stewards on God's behalf. Fourth, it reveals God's plan of love and forgiveness through Jesus Christ, which God established before the foundation of the world. And finally, the Bible tells us how to relate to our creator and to our fellowman.[5]

Failure to acknowledge that we do have a "blueprint for living" and failure to apply that blueprint lies at the root of all our problems. Too often we follow the adage, "When all else fails, read the directions." How do we know what God thinks or says about an issue if we have not read "The Handbook"?

We need to employ the attitude of the Berean church that received the words of the apostle Paul with great eagerness, "examining the Scriptures daily, to see whether these things were so."[6] Obedience to God's holy, inspired, inerrant Word leads to wisdom and insight not only about our personal lives, but also about society.[7]

Tragically, most people feel that appealing to scriptural principle is old fashioned and outdated. Yet the Bible has weathered the storms of the past and the present and stands true as our standard for life and living for the future.

Confidence in God's Word

It is of paramount importance that we have confidence in the accuracy and the authority of God's Word, for without that objective, absolute, trustworthy standard, we are left to our own fallen reasonings and speculations.

The Bible itself testifies to its authoritative and instructional character. The apostle Paul writes to a young disciple named Timothy, "All Scripture is inspired by God and profitable for teaching, for reproof, for correction, for training in righteousness; that the man of God may be adequate, equipped for every good work."[8] Jesus proclaimed, "The Scripture cannot be broken,"[9] and He Himself quoted freely from the Old Testament, thus endorsing it as authoritative.

The Bible has proven its reliability in a number of ways. For example, it claims for itself to be the inspired Word of God. The Christian church down through the centuries, regardless of denomination or affiliation, has claimed the Bible to be the Word of God. It is unique in many ways. It contains sixty-six books written by forty different authors over a period of 1,400 years in various parts of Asia, Africa and Europe, in various literary forms, and in three languages. Yet it is one Book. It amazingly retains its unity and internal consistency—it does not contradict itself.

It dares to speak of the future with explicit detail that no other ancient writings have ventured to undertake. More than three hundred prophecies concerning the Messiah of the Old Testament were uniquely fulfilled in Jesus of Nazareth. Science and archaeology have time and time again validated its accuracy in all matters of human life and creation on which it speaks. Equally amazing is the fact that the Bible has repeatedly validated ancient history. Perhaps the most unique aspect of the Bible is its ability to influence individuals and societies throughout history and around the world.

Certainly the Bible stands alone as a guiding light to provide the answers to basic questions that are essential to man's understanding of himself and his world. Such questions are: Who am I? Where did I come from? Where am I going? Is there any purpose in human existence? Where is history going? Only as these essential questions of existence are answered are we in a position to address other issues and situations that confront us today.

"NO, NO, WORLEY. WHEN I SAID GUARD THE ABORTION CLINIC SO NOBODY WOULD GET KILLED, I MEANT ARREST BOMBERS, NOT ABORTIONISTS!"

Analyze and Understand the Issues of Our Day

In everything we hear, view, and read, we should ask questions: What is the source of information? What are its potential biases? What is the underlying world view? If the information comes from an individual, what is his or her moral character? What are the surface implications? What is the root issue underlying all the symptoms? We need to logically analyze the information we receive, rather than blindly accept all that is presented to us. An excellent way to do this is to try to determine the world view of the person or persons presenting the information.

James Sire explains this concept well in his book, *How to Read Slowly:*

> When writers write they do so from the perspective of their own world view. What they presuppose about themselves, God, the good life and the validity of human knowledge governs both what they say and how they say it. That is why reading with world views in mind (your own and that of the author) will help you understand not only what is written in the lines but what is written between the lines—that is, what is presupposed before a pen ever reaches the page.[10]

Compare Your Analysis With Scripture

What does the Bible have to say? If you do not know, you need to study it to find out. Locate and list the words in the Bible that are synonomous with your topic. You may need to consult a concordance, Bible dictionary, or topical Bible. Look also for stories or teaching passages in which the topic is discussed or illustrated in depth.

Then group the verses and passages that have a common theme. List specific Bible commands or prohibitions. Look for biblical principles that go beyond the cultural or historical context of the Scripture passages. Finally, attempt to summarize your tentative understanding of the biblical perspective in one paragraph, or in a list of biblical principles.

Now, compare your findings with the issue you are studying. Examine presuppositions, realizing that no one is totally objective. Everyone makes decisions through a grid of beliefs, understandings and personal standards of truth and non-truth.

You may want to go further and examine other sources such as Christian periodicals, books, and organizations specializing in a particular issue or topic. We have listed some of the best in the back of this book. Evaluate various positions and attempt to understand them. How do they match the biblical standard? Look for areas of agreement and non-agreement. Critique, reject, accept, or adapt the conclusions of others. If you do not agree with their conclusions, try to develop arguments in response, dealing as much as possible with presuppositions in order to show that the logical extension of wrong foundations results in wrong conclusions.

Apply the Biblical Perspective

Jesus said that if we loved Him, we would obey His commandments. Biblical knowledge without obedience does nothing more than promote spiritual pride. We need to be obedient to the truths of Scripture. Demonstrate by your own life the proper biblical practice before you apply it to a broader audience.

We must remember that we are to love those who are wrong, while gently but firmly refuting their positions. Set *a solution goal* that will provide a consistent practice of biblical principles. It may be slow. We need to realize there will be resistance to change. We do not want to polarize or antagonize people unnecessarily.

As you make application, evaluate the process and adjust as necessary. Evaluate the role of the Holy Spirit— is He the one directing you? If a problem precipitated your investigation, establish preventive steps for its recurrence. Establish policy guidelines for similar issues and problems you may face in the future and follow through consistently, without partiality.

Fill Your Mind With Healthy Food

One activity in particular will aid us greatly in achieving a biblical world view. Today we are experiencing an explosion of secular knowledge. We need to balance that input by doing as the apostle Paul commanded, "Set your mind on the things above, not on the things that are on earth."[11] That is best done through meditation. This is not the eastern kind popularized by Transcendental Meditation. Eastern forms of meditation encourage people to focus on nothing, or within themselves, or on a universal power or force, or on some seemingly meaningless word.

The biblical concept of meditation is the idea of "chewing" as a sheep chews its cud. When we meditate on God and His Word, we experience three things: intimacy with God; a renewed mind as Christ's thoughts become our thoughts; and changed behavior. As we meditate on Scripture, we allow God's thoughts to so permeate our lives that they actually become our own thoughts, resulting in new behavior patterns and eventually in changed emotions.

The following are some suggestions for biblical meditation:[12]

1. Schedule time, preferably daily, to be alone so that you can concentrate.

2. Select a verse or passage, one that when internalized will help you in a specific area, such as a besetting sin, a weakness, an area you have selected for growth, or an issue in your profession.

3. Study the passage in context.

4. Memorize. You do not have to memorize verses in order to begin meditation, but memorization will significantly aid the process of internalization.

5. Visualize—make the truth of Scripture as vivid in your mind as possible. Those in the field of mass media understand the power of visualization: It helps viewers to see a life-style or product they want us to buy. We need to do the same with spiritual truth. As an athlete visualizes himself performing in a sports event, we need to mentally picture ourselves winning the spiritual battles of the day. It is not the visualization that produces the results. The visualization, rather, adds to our concentration, our understanding and our dedication to obeying and trusting in God's Word.

6. Personalize the Scripture passage and make it a prayer to God.

7. Take time to be quiet, to listen to what God has to say to you.

8. Take action, applying the commands and principles of Scripture to your life.

Jerry Nims was director of several multi-national corporations. As a Christian, he had never seriously thought about the concept of Jesus Christ as the Lord of his life. A meeting with the late Francis Schaeffer caused him to re-evaluate his business practices and priorities in light of his faith.

In order to formulate his own world view, Jerry stepped down from his position and spent six months studying the Scriptures from Genesis to Revelation nine to ten hours every day. "When I finished that project, I was prepared to go back into the business arena," he says.

> "The time I spent studying the Bible had a dramatic influence on every area of my life. For example, I decided to do some things to help improve society, based on a biblical world view. If we don't have more businessmen working to shore up the moral framework of society, when it collapses, nobody will do business."[13]

Not everyone can take a six-month break, but nearly everyone could take a week or more each year and some time daily to get away from the pressures of business and study the Scriptures for the purpose of clarifying his world view. We must not rely on others to do this for us. If we do nothing, others will lead us where we do not want to go. The battle against Satan begins here, with ideas, with our minds. How we do in every other area will be determined by how we do here. See Appendixes A and D for further information.

Summary

- Mere human viewpoints must be challenged by God's viewpoint as found in the Bible.
- We need to analyze and understand the issues of our day from a biblical perspective.
- We need to apply our biblical perspective to the issues that confront us.
- Biblical meditation is an essential aid to developing a consistent biblical world and life view.

ACTION STEP

Do you think biblically? Take an issue you are presently facing and apply the biblical thinking process.

1. Analyze and understand the issue.
2. Compare your analysis with the Scripture.
3. Apply your biblical perspective to the issue.

What is your biggest besetting personal problem?

_____

_____

Find a Scripture that relates to it.

_____

_____

Apply the section on meditation. Meditate four times daily on that Scripture, for one week. Check the difference in your attitude and approach to the problem.

_____

_____

8

BOOT CAMP:

Back to the Basics

"I hope I didn't humiliate you, letting you beat me only two out of three games," Ron gasped as Greg and he sat in the sauna at the racquetball club following their match. After a few moments of sitting in that pine-covered "frying pan," the conversation turned to a discussion about leadership, a favorite topic of theirs.

In the middle of this interaction, Russ, a third man in the sauna, commented from his sprawled-out position on the bench, "The best way to get back at a leader is to dig around in his garbage."

Ron and Greg glanced bewilderedly at one another, and Ron responded, "Why do you want to look in a guy's garbage can?"

"Not garbage *can*, but garbage. You know, dirty linen, problems, dirt...you know!" retorted Russ.

Having learned many years before that this kind of "off the wall" discussion was a prime introduction into spiritual issues, Ron turned the discussion that way and said, "I have enough problems with my own dirt and it doesn't excite me to try to exploit anyone else's."

"I guess I know what you mean," Russ concurred half-heartedly.

But then he went on to waddle through a quagmire

of the most filthy phrases about human beings that Ron and Greg had heard in a long time: "You can't trust most b————!" "They can all go to h——." And much, much more, ad nauseum.

Ron grabbed the discussion back, thinking he had a real live pagan with a need for Christ. "Most of us would be a mess, if God weren't so gracious to us. I know I would be," he responded.

Expecting a silence or questioning response after God was brought into the conversation, Ron and Greg were both a bit surprised to hear Russ's response.

"Amen," declared Russ boldly. "I would be a mess too, if I didn't know God!"

"You know God?" stuttered Greg.

"Oh yeah, I'm a born-again Christian!" proclaimed Russ confidently.

"Are you a brand-new Christian?" Ron queried.

"Oh no, I've been a Christian since 1971. And then, I recommitted my life to Jesus in 1975, after my divorce. And, since then, I've been a leader in numerous Christian ministries. God has been really doing a lot in my life in the last two years."

"It's too hot in here for me," Ron said.

"Me too," responded Greg. "We'll see you around the club and talk some more, Russ."

"Great!" answered Russ.

Afterward, all Ron and Greg could do was look at each other in disbelief. Unfortunately, this experience typifies much of Christianity in America today.

"Too harsh!" you retort. Is it really? How many Christians are there who claim to be "born again" or who have "received Christ," but manifest little, if any, life-changing power? How easy is it to tell a Christian from a non-Christian? If fifty-nine million adults in America claim to be born again, why is our society disintegrating?

This is not a problem, it is a plague! And the solution must begin with some basic training for new Christians. In fact, the body of Christ needs to call Christians back to boot camp.

We Christians can supply the information and talk

the lingo like Russ. But, where are the changed lives? Apparently most Christians have skipped over, have ignored, or have not been exposed to the fundamentals of the Christian life. Many Christians currently training younger believers need to go back and learn the basics themselves. The author of Hebrews realized the same problem in Hebrews 5:11-15:

> Concerning him [Melchizedek] we have much to say, and it is hard to explain, since you have become dull of hearing. For though by this time you ought to be teachers, you have need again for some one to teach you the elementary principles of the oracles of God, and you have come to need milk and not solid food. For every one who partakes only of milk is not accustomed to the word of righteousness, for he is a babe. But solid food is for the mature, who because of practice have their senses trained to discern good and evil.

God's Word, in 1 John 2:1-5, says that those who truly love God will obey and please Him.[1]

Rebuild the Foundations: Learn to Think Biblically

But where do we begin? What are the basics? In light of the commission we have to reach the world for Christ, we must work backward to determine what foundations must exist for us to be successful.

For instance, we cannot penetrate our world as salt and light unless we are loving people sacrificially.[2] Furthermore, such love flows out of a holy life, submitted to Christ.[3] Finally, holy living flows from biblical thinking.

Thus, our basic training must begin with our thinking and flow to our ministry. First, *Christian leaders must begin by teaching people how to think biblically*, instead of humanistically. As Jesus prayed in John 17, we are to be "sanctified in truth."

Someone once said, "It's not what we think we are. It's what we think, we are." Since we are so deeply influenced by what we think, it is vital for Christians to refocus their thought patterns. We need to think more clearly about such items as the primacy and significance of the Word of God. For, if the Bible is true, we *must* study and obey it. If it is not true, we ought to discount it. We cannot afford to merely *think* it is true. We must believe it, be convinced about it and act like it. But because we do not do this, most Christians live like atheists.[4]

Second, *we must turn to the Bible as our basis for guidance.* Too often, Christians make decisions on the basis of statements like: "Others do it that way," or "We've always done it that way," or "It works best that way," or "It's the easiest way," or "This way will make me'most happy." We Christians are getting highly conformed to the world system[5] because of this weak thinking. We must become biblically discerning.

Third, *we need to learn what the Bible means when it calls us a "new creature in Christ."* We are *not* to live in the old kingdom of darkness anymore. We are children of the light. We need to walk that truth. But first, we need to understand that when we truly receive Christ as our Lord and Savior we do indeed become new creatures.

Fourth, *we need to expand our view of God.* So often, our "problems" seem so big because, as J. B. Phillips put it, "Your God is too small." We tend to box God in. We must see Him as the great, awesome, powerful person He is. We must explode our narrow presuppositions about Him.

Fifth, *we must rethink our purpose on the earth.* Most Christians would willingly say we are here to glorify God—love Him, obey Him and witness for Him. But, do we live for eternity? Are our values heaven centered? Do we live with the knowledge that time is precious? Are we available for and being used by God to make an impact on others and on our society? Or are we just existing? Are we living like those around us? Are we giving part of ourselves to the Lord, but not everything?

Finally, in the area of thinking biblically, *we must sharpen our thoughts about spiritual warfare.* Christians are not living as though they are at war. We are living rather passively in a comfortable, affluent culture. Some believe that God may need to bring the United States to financial collapse or political overthrow in order to shake us from our self-sufficient apathy so that He can really use us for His glory.

In any event, we have been dulled and softened. It is time to get back onto warfare footing. That means life *not* as usual. It means "tearing down the fortresses" of Satan. It means boldness, commitment, sacrifice and penetration. It means victory.

Learn to Live Righteously

Once Christians have learned to think biblically, leaders must move on to the second major priority, which is to train Christians in how to live righteously. The world is crying out for holy, righteous, godly men and women. Our tendency today is to move away from personal righteousness and, as a result, to move away from societal and corporate righteousness. We must help men and women to understand once again what is involved in personal holiness.

It is helpful to remember that the word *holiness* is the same word as *sanctification* in the New Testament. *Sanctification* means "set aside for a special purpose or service." The reality of that was driven home to Ron one day when he walked into the kitchen of a friend's home and saw the wife picking up freshly baked chocolate chip cookies and looking at the bottom of them.

She was saying under her breath, "John, guest, John, John, guest, John, guest, guest, guest, John." Every time she looked at the bottom of a cookie, she had to put it in a "John" (her husband) pile or a "guest" pile. When Ron asked her what she was doing, she said, "Oh, I'm giving all the good ones to the guests and I'm putting all the ones that are burnt in this pile for John to eat."

Well, those were sanctified cookies. They were being set aside for their special purpose. In the same way, when we put an emphasis on holiness, we must realize that we need to be retrained to understand that holiness is not just being separate *from sin*, but being set apart *to God*. That means we need to be men and women who are quick to deal with sin in our own lives as well as being sensitive to sin in society. We must be committed to allowing God to break, mold and use us for His intended purpose.

Learn to Love Supernaturally

The third major priority of retraining is that of learning to love supernaturally. It is one thing to think biblically and live righteously, but unless that is being realized on a day-to-day basis in supernatural loving, we will never fulfill God's purpose for us on this earth.

John 17 records our Lord Jesus Christ's prayer. He could have prayed anything, but He prayed that we would be sanctified in truth (that we would think biblically and live righteously.) He went on to pray in verse 23 that we would "be perfected in unity" so that the world might know that the Father sent His Son into the world and that the Father loves His children.

You see, the greatest evangelistic tool we have today is the love we have one for another. We need to manifest this kind of love in the Body of Christ and toward the non-believing world. Yet today the tendency is to become more and more geared around our cliques and our narrow perspectives. That is not the biblical perspective. In fact, what we need is the kind of unity that Juan Carlos Ortiz calls "mashed potato love" in his book *Disciple*.[6]

He uses the analogy of potatoes to illustrate the unity of Christian love. For instance, you put potatoes in the ground and they may grow together, but there is no unity. So you take them out of the ground and put them in a bucket. Now they are touching, and there is still no unity. So you take those potatoes out of the bucket, wash them off, and put them in a strainer so that they are touching skin to skin. Yet there is still no unity.

Next you take those potatoes out of the strainer and peel off the skin and put them together. Now they are touching with the facade gone but still there is no unity. And so you slice the potatoes and dice them and intermix them but there is still no unity. There is only one way to get unity out of those potatoes. That's right! You must put them in boiling water until they are ready to be mashed. That is the only way they become a unit.

In a similar manner, God allows His children to be

tested by the heat and pressures of life, so that we might learn the unifying nature of Christian love. That will never happen until we die to ourselves and put others first. Although we retain our individual uniqueness, the Lord Himself prayed that we might be one in love as a witness to the world.

Learn to Penetrate Strategically

The fourth and final quality that we need to see in the area of retraining is a strategic penetration. In John 17, Jesus prayed that His followers would exhibit such a dramatic love that the world would know that the Father had sent the Son. In other words, our biblical thinking should reflect itself in righteous living, which, in turn, reflects itself in sacrificial loving, which then penetrates our society. We are to be salt and light, as Jesus stated in Matthew 5.

"You are the salt of the earth." In ancient times, salt was a valuable commodity and in some cases used as money, a medium of exchange. But a simple consideration reveals the nature and value of salt. First and foremost, it was used as a preservative in a society without refrigeration. It helped retard putrification of foods, especially meats. In like manner we, as Christians, are to retard or halt the decadent trends of an unregenerate society. We should not blame the meat for spoiling if we do not bother to salt it. Ours is a preservative role.

Second, salt has always been used as a seasoning for foods, to enhance or draw out the flavor. We must realize that to season a pound of beefsteak we do not need a pound of salt. In like manner, we do not need large numbers to affect society positively. Just a few committed Christians, willing to live pure lives and apply biblical truth to a particular issue, *can* make a difference. Despite numerous polls that indicate a large percentage of Americans claim to be "born again," we don't often see the positive flavoring of Christians in our own society.

Third, salt can create a thirst. This too is the function of a believer. He should live in such a manner that the unbeliever will desire to know why he has hope in a hopeless world.[7]

"You are the light of the world." Light shows the way; it gives light to a path. We live in a spiritually dark world. Jesus has commanded us to let our lights so shine that men may see our good works and glorify our Father who is in heaven. How many of us live a life-style that differs much from our non-Christian neighbor? Oh, he sees us go to church on Sunday while he is washing his car or mowing his lawn. But, apart from our church activities, does he see anything different in the way we discipline our children or speak to our spouse when frustrated? No, light in the darkness draws attention. Light and darkness are mutually exclusive. You cannot have both at the same time. Jesus said the darkness cannot overcome the light.[8] We must *not* hide our light. Let it shine! Let it penetrate the darkness!

Light exposes hidden things. Sometimes we do not want to be exposed as Adam and Eve were in the Garden of Eden following the fall. We recoil and seek to hide from the light. That is also the reaction of the non-Christian, in many cases, when he is around a radiant believer. Do you make people uncomfortable when you are around? Is it because you are so strange or sober, or is it because your life so reflects the True Light—Jesus Christ? There are times when we actively need to confront the deeds of darkness and expose sin individually and collectively. Is your light repelling or attracting or confronting?

We want to be the light that leads people to the one who said, "I am the Way, the Truth, and the Life."[9] He is the same one who promised, "I am the Light of the world. So if you follow me, you won't be stumbling through the darkness, for living light will flood your path."[10]

As we demonstrate holiness, godliness, and biblical goodness and kindness through our lives, and proclaim the realities of Jesus Christ and the validity and absoluteness of biblical truth, we will be penetrating strategically.

Furthermore, as we seek to conserve the areas of goodness in our society and then go on to reclaim for Christ major areas of our society, we will certainly be moving toward doing what God has called us to do by way of strategic penetration.

Later, we will discuss how Christians can amplify the basic conceptual truths examined in this chapter on basic training. The point is that we need to begin to move aggressively now if we are going to fulfill the purpose for which God has placed us on this earth.

That will happen only as we get back to basic training which creates the conceptual and practical framework in which we can build the rest of our Christian lives and impact.

Summary

- We must retrain our minds to think biblically.
- We must use the Bible as the basis for guidance.
- We must live as a "new creature in Christ."
- We need to expand our view of who God is.
- We need to rethink our view of our purpose on earth: personal peace and comfort, or glorifying God?
- We need to live and think as if we were at war—spiritual war with Satan's kingdom.

ACTION STEP

Evaluate your foundation:

I think biblically.

> Poor Average Good Excellent

I live righteously.

> Poor Average Good Excellent

I love supernaturally.

> Poor Average Good Excellent

I penetrate my sphere of influence strategically.

> Poor Average Good Excellent

9

THE REVOLUTIONARY LIFE-STYLE:

Preparation for Battle

The story is told of an illiterate farmer from the rural Midwest who, during the early stages of World War II, heard about the attack on Pearl Harbor. Motivated by a love for his country, he immediately left the farm with his wife and headed to the West Coast to work in the shipyards. His wife found work as a waitress to support them.

Unable to read, the farmer did not understand the meaning of the slip of paper he received once a week at the shipyard. It was not until he had accumulated several thousand dollars in checks that he learned that he was being paid to help save his country.[1]

That farmer was committed to doing his part to help save his country, and he assumed that meant sacrificing. The Communists understand that concept, and they have a slogan that summarizes their commitment: "dead men on furlough." As much as anything, that explains their phenomenal success.

Bill once met with the new president of a country where the Communists had previously been making great strides in taking over. Bill congratulated the president for his success in pushing back the Communists and asked what he thought about the future of communism in that country.

"I'm not optimistic," he said. "They never give up. Ultimately they will succeed in taking over the country."

The Communists have made steady gains throughout the world because they believe no sacrifice, even death, is too great for the advancement of their ideology.

Total Commitment

Why is it that Communists seem to have a far higher level of commitment than most Christians? The reason is that the Communist Party constantly reminds its members that they are fulfilling a dream that is far greater than the individual. The goal is that everything the individual party member does—his every waking moment, his every action—is geared toward the fulfillment of the dream.

But the original "dead man on furlough" is the Galatians 2:20 Christian: "I am crucified with Christ, but nevertheless I live, yet not I, but Christ liveth in me and the life I now live in the flesh, I live by faith in the Son of God who loved me and gave Himself for me." This calls us to a total commitment to Christ and His lordship that the Communists cannot hope to copy.

Bill was meeting at Harvard with one of America's great statesmen to share a plan to involve a thousand key leaders in praying for, claiming and supporting the goal of reaching one billion souls for Christ before the year 2000. The man responded, "I don't wear my religion on my sleeve. My religion is personal and private, and I don't talk about it?"

Bill was taken aback by this very forthright rejection and asked the man if he was a Christian. "Yes, I am. But I am not a fanatic."

"Did it ever occur to you that it cost Jesus Christ His life so that you could say you're a Christian?" Bill asked. "And it cost the disciples their lives. Millions of Christians throughout the centuries have suffered and died in order to get the message of God's love and forgiveness to you. Now do you really believe that your faith in Christ is personal and private and you shouldn't talk about it?"

"No sir," the man replied. "I'm wrong. Tell me what I can do about it."

J. B. Phillips understood this truth when he wrote the introduction to his modern English paraphrase of the epistles:

> The great difference between present-day Christianity and that of which we read in these letters is that to us it is primarily a performance, to them it was a real experience. We are apt to reduce the Christian religion to a code, or at best a rule of heart and life. To these men it is quite plainly the invasion of their lives by a new quality of life altogether. They do not hesitate to describe this as Christ "living in" them....We are practically driven to accept their own explanation, which is that their little human lives had, through Christ, been linked up with the very life of God.
>
> ...It is heartening to remember that this faith took root and flourished amazingly in conditions that would have killed anything less vital in a matter of weeks. These early Christians were on fire with the conviction that they had become, through Christ, literally sons of God; they were pioneers of a new humanity, founders of a new Kingdom. They still speak to us across the centuries. Perhaps if we believed what they believed, we might achieve what they achieved.[2]

Why should the commitment of the Christian be any less today than it was in the first century? We are citizens in the kingdom of light. Ours is the greatest and only worthwhile cause. God has literally called us to go and win the world, to make disciples of all nations, teaching them to obey all that He has commanded. The reason our nation is not greatly influenced by Christianity is that so few of us have the revolutionary life-style necessary to make an impact.

Art DeMoss was a man who believed. During his lifetime he built up a phenomenally successful insurance company, yet his real accomplishments lay in the commitment he had to introducing people to Jesus. Everywhere he went he told waiters, cab drivers and businessmen about his Lord and led thousands to faith in Christ.

Art and Bill were having dinner one evening in Cuernavaca, Mexico. As they were chatting together, the maître d' came over and inquired if they were satisfied with the food and service. Art immediately seized the opportunity to explain that he was in Cuernavaca to speak at an evangelistic campaign in a local church. He asked the maître d' if he was a Christian. The man confessed that he was not. Art then proceeded to witness to him and within a few minutes the man bowed his head and prayed with Art as he received Christ.

Even before Art DeMoss became very successful in his business ventures, even when the assets and liabilities of his business were probably matched at a low figure, Art would speak at evangelistic meetings and was willing to take time away from his business to introduce others to Christ.

The secret to the success of Art DeMoss in business and in witnessing for the Lord lay in the fact that, no matter what happened in his daily schedule, no matter how crowded his agenda for the day, he arose early in the morning and spent at least an hour with the Lord in prayer and reading the Scriptures.

His home was used to introduce fellow executives to Christ. He hosted dinners, often with several hundred guests on his back lawn, and brought in well-known Christian athletes, executives and government officials to share the gospel. Literally thousands of people were introduced to Christ through his ministry, and though he passed away in 1978, his impact continues to be felt today through his wife, Nancy, and their seven children, all of whom are dedicated to Christ.

Supernatural Is Not Natural

The life-style of the early church leaders is the life-style God wants for all of us. But the only way we can achieve it is by living supernaturally.

To do that, *we must first think supernaturally*. That means we need to learn to think the way God thinks, and the only way to do that is to think biblically. We need to recognize how great God truly is. We need to dwell on His attributes and gain confidence in His great power and love. We need to recognize that we are men and women of destiny—there is royal blood in our veins. Because of who God is and who we are, we have incredible power and authority, far greater than any in Satan's kingdom.

Second, *this lifestyle calls for us to pray supernaturally*. We need to experience the truth of Christ's words when He said, "If you abide in Me and my words abide in you, ask whatever you will and it shall be done for you."[3] We have authority over the forces of evil, and Satan and his forces *cannot* prevail against us.

Bill has a dear friend who is as common as clay—not brilliant, eloquent, handsome or especially outgoing—but he is a revolutionary for God. The first time Bill met him, this man had just witnessed to one of the top leaders in America. The circumstances of his meeting with this leader were phenomenal, because God obviously orchestrated it. This is a man whose source of power is prayer. He spends a couple of hours a day in meaningful prayer, not just ritualistic mouthing of words or phrases, but personal conversation with the omnipotent creator, the God of the universe. His revolutionary, supernatural quality is that he lives a holy life, walks in the Spirit, spends much time in the Word and in prayer. Anyone who spends much time with God will be a revolutionary follower of Jesus Christ.

Since this man met with this leader, we have observed that this leader's decisions are more compatible with a biblical world view.

Third, *we need to plan supernaturally*. Asking God to direct us, we must make plans so magnificent, so big, so far beyond mere human accomplishment that we are doomed to failure unless God is at work in us.

Does it make sense to build houses and sell them with no profit margin at zero percent interest? Perhaps not in our society, but it really makes sense to Millard Fuller.

The fourty-nine-year-old Fuller began his business career while in high school. In college he started several businesses, and by the age of twenty-nine he was a self-made millionaire. But, he was not pleased with his success and relates in an interview:

> "Because of a domestic crisis, my wife and I decided to com-
> pletely change our lives and to seek after what God wanted us
> to do. We decided that when we left the business, that if we
> were serious about changing our lives and following God that
> we should make ourselves totally available for those purposes
> and get rid of anything that would obstruct us from being free
> and able to do God's work. So I sold my interest in the company
> to my former partner and donated literally one-hundred percent
> of the money to various Christian ventures."[4]

In place of a business empire, Fuller formed a program called Habitat for Humanity, based on what he
called biblical economics. The firm builds homes for the
poor, charging no profit and no interest, and allows people
twenty years to pay. No government funds are used, but
Fuller challenges people to donate money, materials and
time. One of his recruits is former President Jimmy Car-
ter.

"We say that we use the economics of Jesus," says
Fuller. "We believe that if you move on faith, God moves
with you. Our long-range goal is to eliminate poverty
housing in the world. Now that's an audacious, outrage-
ous goal and everybody says 'You must be crazy!...' But
I happen to be a professing Christian. The Bible I read
says that, 'With God all things are possible.'"[5]

Fourth, *we need to love supernaturally.* Jesus told His
disciples to love each other "just as much as I have loved
you. Your strong love for each other will prove to the
world that you are my disciples."[6] Such love is humanly
impossible, for He loved us enough to die for each one of
us. But, the fruit of the Holy Spirit is love. As we allow
the Spirit to control us, love is a natural result.

Fifth, *we need to live supernaturally.* Before He left
this earth, Jesus promised that He would send a helper,
the Holy Spirit, to live within each believer. The Spirit
teaches us about God, provides supernatural peace, guides
us into all truth, and empowers us to carry out His commands.

In order to live supernaturally, we must walk by
faith. We are the ones who decide, as an act of the will,

whether to live supernaturally. It is a choice, based on God and what He tells us in His Word. We exercise faith when we choose to act on what He says. Faith increases through use. The more we choose to trust God, the more we will believe Him and the more faith we will have to trust Him for the next situation.

But there is one more point that incorporates all of supernatural living. In fact, it is the ultimate demonstration of supernatural living: becoming a bondslave of Jesus Christ.

Bondslave for Jesus Christ

The greatest experience of Bill's life occurred in 1951 when he and his wife, Vonette, chose to become slaves of Jesus Christ, turning over ownership of their lives and all of their possessions to Him. Bill and Vonette had to face up to the challenge of the Lord Jesus when He said, "Seek first the kingdom of God and His righteousness," and "Lay up treasures in heaven, don't lay them up on earth where moth and rust corrupt or thieves break through and steal."[7]

"I was a very materialistic person, and so was my wife," Bill says. "We had luxurious appetites. I was in business for myself, enjoyed the good life, had great prospects for a life of exceptional success. I manufactured fancy foods, was involved in leasing, drilling and producing oil in the Midwest and was already experiencing considerable success. I planned to give a good percentage of my profits to the Lord.

"But the Lord led Vonette and me, in the spring of 1951, to sign a contract with Him, whereby we formally became slaves of Jesus Christ, just as Paul speaks of in Romans 1:1. We chose to sign a contract relinquishing all of our rights to Him. We would never seek the praise or applause of men, labor for material wealth or pursue the worldly life-style that had once been so important to us. It was our goal simply to be slaves of Jesus Christ the rest of our lives, to do whatever He wanted us to do, to go wherever He wanted us to go, whatever the cost, and say whatever He wanted us to say.

"It was soon after that commitment that God revealed the vision that led to the formation of Campus Crusade for Christ. I do not believe that God would have entrusted me with the vision for this ministry had there not first been our total surrender to the lordship of Christ."

Many of us have no problem considering ourselves servants of God. But slaves—that is a different matter. Yet there are some distinct advantages to being a slave as opposed to being a servant.

A servant is paid a wage, though sometimes it is not a great amount. With that money, he is free to do what he wishes, but he also has the responsibility for obtaining his own food, shelter, clothing and any other possessions.

A slave, however, is not paid any wage. The master is responsible for providing all that the slave needs. The slave has no responsibility except to do what the master tells him to do. The master may reward him for a job well done, and sometimes that turns out to be more than a servant would have earned. But the slave never expects such blessing.

The servant works a certain number of hours, and then he has his own time to do as he pleases. The slave is always at the call of his master. His time is never his own, but whatever the master desires, the slave gladly obliges.

One might wonder why anyone would want to be a slave. The apostle Paul considered himself a slave and derived great joy from that. The word he used several times is actually translated "bondslave." In the Hebrew law, a slave was required to be freed after seven years of service. If he liked the master, however, and wanted to continue working for him, the slave had the master pierce his ear. Thus he became a bondslave and remained his master's possession for life.[8]

The key is that the bondslave *chose* to be a slave. And so it is with God. Jesus challenged His disciples, "If any one wishes to come after Me, let him deny himself, and take up his cross, and follow Me."[9] Paul, because of the overwhelming love God showed him, chose to become

God's slave. That same opportunity awaits us.

It is interesting to note that Jesus warns against the possibility of having two masters: "No one can serve two masters; for either he will hate the one and love the other, or he will hold to one and despise the other." But notice how Jesus specifically applies this idea: "You cannot serve God and mammon."[10] Mammon means wealth or profit that becomes the center of life instead of God. The slave has to choose which master he will serve.

Adventurous Life-style

Being a slave to Christ is the most exciting, adventurous life-style available today. Bob Davenport, a former All-American football player at UCLA, would tell you that.

Bill had the privilege of discipling and working closely with Bob for four years while he was in college. Bob still stands out as one of the most remarkable young men that Bill has ever known. Bob was inspired with the Christian life primarily because of a woman who took him into her home as a son when he was a teenager and made him a part of her family. "The bombardment of her love in keeping house, making my lunches and caring for me as if I were one of her own children made me want to identify spiritually with her and her family," Bob says.[11]

As he graduated from college and played professional football, Bob found himself speaking often to youngsters who complained that nothing exciting ever happened in their churches. "In 1963, I felt God telling me to give the summer to working with kids." He spent those months camping, playing, and building friendships with teenage youth, and as he did, he developed the idea of taking kids on long-distance bicycle trips. The result was Wandering Wheels, an organization that has taken thousands of youngsters on long-distance bike trips, including twenty-seven coast-to-coast tours. During these weeks on the road, Bob spends time discipling the youngsters, and their lives are literally revolutionized by the experience.

"I've never been very interested in money," says Bob today. "My most pleasant experiences are investing in lives, and now I receive the dividends of numerous friendships and families around the country that are geared to the Christian life-style."

What does God's bondslave look like? He is anyone who is committed to doing God's will in every area of life—in his business or profession, in his family, in his church, in his neighborhood, and in his world.

Summary

We must live the supernatural life-style by *faith* in the following areas:
- We must think supernaturally and biblically.
- We must pray supernaturally.
- We must plan supernaturally, in dependence on God for direction.
- We need to love supernaturally in the power of the Holy Spirit.
- We need to live supernaturally as slaves of God.

ACTION STEP

Take one area from the above list and commit yourself to living this quality in the next twenty-four hours. Stop hourly and evaluate how you are doing.

10

FAMILY:

The Key Life Support

The traditional American family is undergoing a dramatic change in its life-style. In the book *Vital Signs*, George Barna and William Paul McKay give these startling statistics:

> Just after the turn of the century, in 1910, only one-tenth of one percent of the nation's population (83,000 people) had experienced divorce. Times have changed. In 1982 alone, 1.18 million couples saw their marriages dissolve.[1]

Not only has there been an increase in divorce in general, but the Christian home also has not gone unscathed, as Barna and McKay note:

> At this critical juncture, even the Christian home is feeling the impact of divorce. In 1983 there were ten million born-again Christians who had been divorced at one point in their lives. Marital separation—a step that almost inevitably leads to formal divorce—characterized the lives of an additional one million Christian families.[2]

While Barna and McKay's statistics about divorced Christians do not distinguish whether the divorce occurred before or after the person's salvation, our counseling with thousands of divorced individuals indicates that God has often used the crisis of divorce as a means of drawing individuals to Himself for salvation, or a return from a

STAYSKAL
'85 TAMPA
TRIBUNE

"WHAT A DAY... DID THE LAUNDRY, DROPPED LULU AT SCHOOL, GOT MY HAIR DONE, WENT SHOPPING, GOT A DIVORCE, PICKED UP LULU..."

carnal life-style for those previously saved.

But it is not only the Christian sheep that are having problems; so also are the shepherds. *Vital Signs* quotes a survey that suggests that "the divorce rate among ministers has more than quadrupled since 1960."[3]

Barna and McKay summarize in a most telling way:

> Although Christians believe that marriage is intrinsically an important institution, they are buckling under the social and economic pressures that have challenged marital relationships and child-rearing obligations. Though once deemed a permanent bond between people, these days marriage is more commonly viewed as a union of convenience or expedience.[4]

The Family: A Fortress or a Farce?

By contrast, those Christians who are seriously committed to God as evidenced in their Bible study, prayer and church attendance, experience a high level of marital stability. As a new Christian in 1946, Bill heard his pastor quote statistics concerning marriage that had a profound impact on him. Where as many as one in two-and-a-half marriages ended in divorce at that time, he had found that among husbands and wives who read the Bible and prayed together every day, only one in 1,015 marriages ended in divorce.

More recently, a study by the *Chicago Catholic* found "church attendance and prayer appear to be remedies to divorce. The divorce rate drops from the national average of 50 percent to 1-in-50 among married couples who regularly attend church and 1-in-1,105 among those with active prayer lives in their home."[5]

To end this invasion of worldly thought and action and reverse the trend of cultural accommodation to the world system's ideas on the family, it is important that we understand God's laws for the family, for that is the fortress from which we engage the enemy in battle. This understanding must move into conviction and, ultimately, personal application, if we are to rebuild the God-ordained, foundational, social institution: the family.

Those who help to influence an anti-Christian public opinion have begun a move to redefine what a family is. The new definition for family is, "people who are living together with deep commitment and with mutual needs and sharing."[6]

Notice that this definition does *not* require married mothers and fathers, only people. This could mean people living together without benefit of marriage, homosexuals or lesbians, or any other arrangement you could think of. Thus, the traditional arrangement of the family is minimized.

An article in *Parade* magazine on mothers raising their sons after divorce exemplifies this humanistic view of the family. The final paragraph quotes Dr. Oscar Christensen, professor of counseling and guidance at the University of Arizona in Tucson, who said:

> I would like to explode two myths. One is that every boy needs a dog. The other is that every child should have two parents. All he needs is one good one.[7]

Revolution in Family Living

To rebuild families to glorify God we suggest the following principles as the basis of a revolution in family living.

1. The husband and wife must seek first the kingdom of God, to love Him with all their hearts, minds and souls.

The happiest of marriages occurs when a husband

and wife, individually and together, set their affections on God. They desire above all else to know, love and obey God.

Vonette and Bill made commitments to each other and to God on their knees, many years ago. They prayed, "God, from today onward we want to surrender all our rights to You, to do whatever You want us to do as a couple and as individuals for the rest of our lives." Their signed contract with God was a statement to each other and to God of an absolute, irrevocable commitment to the lordship of Christ in their lives.

Someone has well said in a song, "Friends are friends forever, if the Lord is the Lord of them."

2. Husbands must learn to love their wives as Christ loves the church.

Too often husbands are selfish and inconsiderate; either overbearing, harsh and dictatorial or passive, withdrawn and uninvolved. They fail to demonstrate the 1 Corinthians 13 kind of love to their wives. This becomes evident when a husband does not take the time to communicate with his wife, appreciate her and encourage her. As a result, an alienation sets in that can destroy the marriage. In Ephesians 5:25 God commands husbands to love their wives just as Jesus Christ loves the church.

And how did Christ love the church? He gave Himself for it, to the extent of laying down His life. That kind of love is *constructive*; that is, it is meant to build the church up to complete fulfillment. In the same way, husbands need to build up their wives. A 50/50 proposition will not work because people always feel that they give more than 50 percent. That is the problem with our sin nature. Ron has learned that he can meet his wife's needs by being sensitive to who she is. That may mean washing the dishes, taking care of the kids, providing Mary the opportunity to get away to a hotel for a weekend of rest and reflection, encouraging her to develop her gifts and ministry, and much more. The point is to build her up, not tear her down or even merely co-exist with her.

A second element of Christ's radical love is that it is a *constant*. "Love never fails."[8] It doesn't quit. Ron recently met with a young executive who was contemplating divorce. In fact, he had already filed for divorce. His wife was trying to change her life-style and attitudes to salvage the marriage, but he was so hurt by her previous behavior that he wanted to "hold over her head" the possibility of a divorce.

"How will you know if you should drop the divorce, Mark?" Ron queried.

"I don't know; I guess I'll get a sign from God," Mark answered.

"I'm your sign!" Ron retorted quickly. "You see, God has made it clear, Mark. He hates divorce. He meant marriage to be forever. And, even though there may be some biblical reasons to open the door to divorce, your situation doesn't fit. Even if you had biblical cause, God wants you to continue to love your wife as Christ loved the church. The issue is not whether Betty will change. The issue is not how you feel about her. The issue is, *Will you be obedient to God and His Word now?* You must drop the divorce or admit you are sinning against God. The choice is yours."

"Too harsh!" you say. No, it is God's way. God calls us to a love that is constant; it does not quit when the going gets tough. As Ron went on to explain to Mark, "Aren't you glad God doesn't hold rejection over your head? His grace never quits."

A third element of Christ's love is *completeness.* Jesus went to the cross. He died for us. He gave all He had for us. Men must learn to die for the needs of their wives. Not so that the wives will get life insurance money, but something more expensive—the attention, the time, the concern, the appreciation and the love that men need to give them. You may need to refuse that job transfer, that night out or even your rather frenetic life-style.

A leading pastor told us that he was forced to come to grips with his poor leadership in his home when his wife once asked him after twenty-two consecutive nights out of the home, "Do you *really* need to go? Can't you stay home one night?"

At that, he turned to her and said, "Fine. People are

going to hell all around us! We can help them by doing God's work, and you want me to stay home and hold your hand!" His own statement rebuked him.

Though you might not say it so blatantly, you may be saying it by the priorities of your life. How significant is your wife to you? Will you die to yourself and your own plans for her?[9]

3. Wives must learn how to love their husbands.

There has been a lot of misinformation about the subject of submission. Ephesians 5:22 tells wives to be submissive to their husbands as unto the Lord. That is not a derogatory instruction that puts women into a lower echelon of society. Unfortunately, the influence of our culture has clouded our understanding of what a godly woman is.

When Bill's boys, Zach and Brad, were small, Vonette felt pushed and frustrated because she wanted to involve herself fully in Campus Crusade for Christ. After the children were born, she had to adjust to her new situation and responsibilities. Bill finally said to her, "Honey, if you will make it your priority to keep the house running, and make the boys happy and see that their needs are met, that will be the most important thing you can do now."

That relieved Vonette of a burden, because she realized a time would come when the boys would not need a mother at home and the house would not need a full-time housekeeper; then she could concentrate on her role as a full-time partner with Bill in the ministry of Campus Crusade for Christ.

Since the boys have grown up and left home, Vonette has been able to serve God within Campus Crusade, as well as develop the Great Commission Prayer Crusade, co-chair the International Prayer Assembly in Korea in 1984 and serve on the Lausanne Committee for World Evangelization for ten years. Vonette was content that God had a time and place for her ministry in the home in earlier years with more time of ministry outside the home in later years. God honored her obedience in caring for the needs of her sons and home. Now she has one of the most effective women's ministries in the world today.

4. Parents should love their children, maintaining discipline while not provoking them to anger.

There are many ways to demonstrate this love and discipline. Ron has taken special interest in practically loving his son, Matthew, through training him in Scripture. They regularly study through the book of Proverbs. They took the Living Bible and used colored pens to note what the Proverbs said about various areas: yellow (tongue), red (wisdom/heart), blue (prohibitions/sins), green (good actions). Then Matt went through and categorized all the verses on wisdom. This type of self-learning has established a base for godly conviction in Matt's life.

For instance, when Matt was struggling with a habit of complaining, Ron was able to appeal to Matt's desire to be a "man of wisdom." Together, they did a Bible study on thanksgiving and worked up this acrostic:

Trust God for everything (Philippians 4:6).

Honor the Lord (Revelation 5:13).

Acknowledge God's goodness (1 Corinthians 1:4; Psalm 145).

Never grumble or gripe (Philippians 2:14-15).

Know God's blessings (Psalm 146).

Sing a song of praise (Psalm 149:1).

Give thanks in everything (1 Thessalonians 5:18).

Instantly give thanks (Ephesians 5:20).

Verbalize your praise (1 Corinthians 14:16-19).

Input positive thoughts in your mind (Philippians 4:8).

Need the Holy Spirit (Galatians 5:25; Ephesians 5:18-20).

Grow in gratitude (Philippians 4:8).

This type of preventive training, along with corrective discipline in a warm, affirming atmosphere will assist greatly in building a godly home.

5. Children need to honor their parents.

This is a commandment with a promise.[10] When children honor their parents, God promises that they will prosper and live a long life.

Children honor their parents by obeying them. It is critical that obedience is not only external but also internal. So many Christian children rebel in later years because they never "owned" the truth they spoke. They piggybacked outwardly on their parents' faith. There was outward conformity with no inward reality and power.

Ron has worked hard constantly to appeal to his children's inward response to the Lord. Recently, Matt "blew up" when Molly, his little five-year-old sister, slammed the door on his nose. This little eight-year-old boy exploded and kicked a hole in the door.

When he came to his senses, his tender little heart was fearful of what Ron might do to discipline him. "Now, I could have disciplined him in a number of ways," Ron says. "But it was clear to me that Matt knew he was wrong, and I wanted to deal with the root issue, anger. So, we did a word study together in the Bible on anger, not as punishment but for constructive growth." As a result, Matt wrote this letter:

Anger

I don't like to be angry. I don't know why I always am. For example: A couple of days ago Molly slamed (sic) the door on me and I got so mad that I kicked the door so hard that it broke. That is why I am doing this paper. I feel ashamed. I now know how really loving God is, putting up with all the bad things we do. I don't know how God can forgive us for all the really terrible things we do.

This type of "broken obedience" is what is meant by "children honoring their parents."

God has established the family as one of the foundational institutions upon which society rests. If the foundation crumbles, the whole of society disintegrates.

These simple "laws" are so basic and yet are so often ignored. Your marriage and family will reflect the King of the "kingdom of light" and so serve as a strong base of operation in the kingdoms at war, if they reflect these principles.

Humanistic View	Biblical View
1. Denies male/female created differences in their nature and role	Acknowledges the God-created differences between men and women
2. Husbands and wives may live independent life-styles under one roof	Husbands and wives should be committed to one another and the primacy of marriage and family
3. Husband pursues career goals while minimizing his family responsibilities	Husband is the shepherd of his family and gives his life for wife and family
4. Wife resists her husband's authority and insists on husband/wife equality in role and authority	Wife joyfully submits to her husband's authority, enjoys his protection and recognizes her equal worth
5. Both will find their primary fulfillment outside the home	Both will find their primary fulfillment within the home
6. Husbands/fathers should provide well for the family but give little personal leadership	Husbands/fathers have responsibilities in spiritual as well as physical ways
7. Parents tend to see children as a liability and an obstacle to fulfilling their own desires	Parents accept children as a gift of God and an opportunity to invest their lives in a future godly generation
8. Parents relegate the upbringing of their children to babysitters, day care centers, television, or leave them without supervision in order to achieve career, materialistic or solely personal goals	Parents will take every possible opportunity to fulfill their responsibility to care for and train their children, love them and shape their character

9. Children have their rights that must be honored	Children have responsibilities of obedience to God and parents
10. Parents should never spank a child; it will make a violent person	Loving discipline helps direct the will of the child to obey the authorities God puts over him

In this comparison chart, the points listed in the humanistic view column are perspectives that persons from a humanist position have expressed. We do not mean to imply that every person claiming to be a humanist would hold to every statement listed.

ACTION STEP

Check each point on the above list that reflects your own life-style. Be honest. Are you pleased with the responses you had to make? What do you need to change?

11

THE CHURCH:

`B´ Company — Believers Only

M uch of Christendom is divided into two camps. One group has dedicated itself to evangelism and discipleship—primarily through emphasis on Bible teaching—and has virtually ignored the social aspects of the gospel. The other camp has focused so much on the social aspects of our faith that it has forgotten Christ's command to go into the world, preach the gospel to all people and make disciples of all nations.

One of Satan's ploys is to try to push us toward one extreme or the other. That inevitably produces divisiveness rather than the unity which God desires in His body. We believe that evangelism and discipleship *and* social involvement are essential. The church needs to become a base camp where individual soldiers can be renewed in order to continue their part in the war effort. It also needs to be a training ground, equipping men and women for ministry. God has designed the local church and the families within it to be His institutions for achieving His ends on this earth. If the church is not healthy—and today it often does lack power and impact—the major influence areas of society will continue to atrophy until society as a whole has no energy to move against evil.

Alexander Horniman, director of the Center for the Study of Applied Ethics at the University of Virginia, points out the lack of health in the church when he says,

> We are asking far less of people today. We don't insist that our older teenagers clean their room or get a job. Schools have fewer language and math requirements. Our churches are trying to make God relevant to people, not vice versa.[1]

The Role of the Church in Spiritual Warfare

Bill is often asked how he would go about building a church. Ron has served as a pastor and is now president of the International School of Theology, training a new generation of ministers who are not only given biblical knowledge, but are also trained in character, convictions and ministry skills. Combining our experience in ministry, we would like to suggest a few ways the church can play a major role in the spiritual warfare that engulfs the world.

1. All of us in the ministry need to be committed to loving God and living holy lives.

God has called us to live our lives totally dependent on Him. He is the one who calls us to minister, and we need to live in obedience to Him by the power of the Holy Spirit. Such lives will be an example to those who follow us. We should include an emphasis on prayer, which needs to permeate every facet of our ministries. We should include an emphasis on evangelism and discipleship. We should be devoted to study of God's word for the purpose of obeying what He has commanded us to do in every area of life. And all that we do should be characterized by love for both God and each other.

Some years ago when Ron finished his doctoral research by touring the country in a twenty-foot motor home with his wife and another couple, he came to some interesting conclusions about the state of the church. After interviewing 300 key Christian leaders in 175 churches in 38 states, he concluded that there was a great zeal for God's *work* but not a passion for *God*.

Ron observed that subtly, Christian leaders, the most influential people in the church, were drifting into a powerless, lifeless existence. There was form but little substance. There was Christian acting but not Christian living. The power and love and joy of intimacy with Christ were seldom experienced.

Intimacy with God and personal holiness must once again become central in the life of the church and her leaders.

2. We should set supernatural goals.

We must not be satisfied with mediocrity or even the best of human achievement. The goals we set should require supernatural intervention and enabling of the Holy Spirit, yet be realistic and obtainable so as not to discourage the leadership and membership of the church.

3. We must warn our people not to ask, "What can I get out of the church?" but rather, "What can I give?"

One of God's laws says that the one who seeks happiness never finds it, but the one who lives to help and serve others finds true fulfillment and meaning in life.

Don Baker, pastor of Hinson Memorial Baptist Church in Portland, Oregon, discovered this truth in a fresh way. He had just preached a sermon from Hebrews 12 on "How to Cope in a Crisis," when a young woman, tears in her eyes, thanked him for the encouragement. She told him how she needed to hear his words after her family had lost their business, home and car and they did not know what they were going to do next.

Pastor Baker suddenly realized that this family needed more than encouragement. They needed help! Immediately! He tells what happened next:

> We announced a special meeting for all the unemployed and underemployed in the church....People from sixty households responded. The enormity of the problem was frightening. We began uncovering needs and seeking out resources, supervised completely by the members of the church. We solicited food, freezers, refrigerators, clothing, and money from the congregation in order to begin an immediate assistance program. I met with the unemployed each Wednesday night to pray and share together, and then a specialist provided counsel in areas such as:
>
> - Finding jobs when they're scarce
> - Preparing resumes
> - Conserving utilities
> - Food shopping on a low income
> - Working with creditors
> - Finding available money
> - What medical assistance was available
> - Government assistance programs
>
> In these meetings we distributed cash for food and emergency needs and made arrangements for clothing and aid in job hunting. Within ninety days we had located most of the hurting.... Through people within the church, we had placed eighty-nine persons in full-time or part-time jobs.[2]

When a person is controlled by Jesus Christ, he begins to see people and situations as Christ sees them. His eyes are opened to the needs and hurts of those around him. And, he is motivated to try to help meet those needs and relieve those hurts. In fact...

4. We need to encourage our congregations to develop a Christian compassion and concern for the poor, illiterate, sick, widows, orphans and prisoners, as our Lord has commanded.

What Pastor Baker started in his church did not end there. People were hurting outside the church, too. A survey of their neighborhood revealed that 70 percent of the population received less than Portland's median income. They mobilized resources with fourteen other churches to reach out into the community and help meet the needs of people in areas as varied as plumbing, auto repairs, babysitting and grocery shopping. As God's love was demonstrated in tangible ways, people naturally came to Christ and the churches grew and prospered.

There is a tendency to expect government to meet the needs of the poor. When we do this, we lose many chances to communicate the message of the gospel, for we are in essence saying that advocates of humanism care more than the church. There are numerous opportunities for churches to be involved in social causes while at the same time furthering the goals of evangelism and discipleship. Various churches across the nation have started day care facilities for abused children, provided homes for families visiting inmates at a nearby prison, operated crisis pregnancy centers for unwed mothers as an alternative to abortion, provided counseling centers for drug and alcohol abusers and victims, and operated "people banks" to provide services for poor and elderly who are unable to afford them.

5. Churches need to penetrate the influence centers of their communities.

One church in Boring, Oregon, has instigated a citizenship class as a part of their adult Sunday school curriculum. Jim Spinks, an elder in Good Shepherd Community Church, explains that the class "covers issues of local, state and national government. We encourage letter writing and local participation. We are doing this because God has not only created the family and the church for His glory, but He also created government. We feel that is one of the areas where we have not spent much time developing biblical perspectives for our people. God has given us the opportunity to say and do a lot about our own government."[3]

Such instruction should help equip church members to run for city council, school board, and local commissions. It should motivate us to take strong public stands for righteousness, perhaps to the point of picketing and boycotting if necessary. It should seek innovative ways to show God's love in action.

Tim LaHaye tells how his wife attended a pro-life meeting in San Diego and realized that there were no members of her church in attendance, even though it was the largest in the city:

> Not only were our ladies absent, but so were women from the other Bible-teaching churches. She met many deeply concerned Catholic ladies, several Mormons, but almost no Protestants. A few days later, one of the humanist leaders of the National Organization for Women (NOW) was quoted as speaking "for the women of America" in her endorsement of the ERA. Bev looked at me and protested, "She doesn't speak for me! And she doesn't represent millions of other women, either." She contacted three other ministers' wives on our staff. The ladies organized a rally, selected five other women, incorporated Concerned Women for America, and launched a national prayer-chain campaign and a monthly newsletter....I have started a number of organizations, all of which enjoy substantial growth, but I have never seen anything like this! The moral-minded women of America are indeed concerned.[4]

The local churches in major population areas need to cover the bases of influence in that area: executives, politicians, media leaders, educators. In fact, every influence area needs to be penetrated. The leaders in the city should be led to Christ, discipled and assimilated into healthy churches. Then they must reproduce this impact strategically among their peers. Furthermore, these leaders and their institutions must be influenced morally. Biblical principles must be winsomely communicated.

The churches must also penetrate society by caring for the poor, the orphans, the widows and others in need, such as women with "problem pregnancies." Love and compassion must be put into "shoe leather" in response to God's love.

One large church may fill several or all of these needs in its locale. Perhaps a few churches will form a coalition to "cover the bases." In any event, action must be taken. If churches do not act, no change will take place.

There is no limit to the potential of the church when it creatively helps God's people reach their maximum effectiveness in the war against Satan's kingdom. Without this commitment on the part of at least a few local churches in each city within the United States and overseas, the battle will not be won. *The church must once again be the church!*

Humanistic View	Biblical View
1. The church is a repressive anachronism today	The church is a foundational institution to society
2. The church is inconsequential to the real world	The church should be salt and light in the middle of this generation
3. The separation of church and state excludes religious influence in any way	The church should have a prophetic role, acting as a watchman for society

In this comparison chart, the points listed in the humanistic view column are perspectives that persons from a humanist position have expressed. We do not mean to imply that every person claiming to be a humanist would hold to every statement listed.

ACTION STEP

Write down one "area of concern" in your immediate community that your church can help to improve.

_____

Brainstorm with one other person on a plan to mobilize some of your church members to have an impact in the area you selected. What first step can you take?

_____

_____

12

MEDIA:

The Window to Our Souls

An executive for one of the major television networks had grown up in a nominal Christian home but was not a practicing Christian. Then he was confronted with the person of Jesus Christ and willingly surrendered his life to Him. In a desire to know more about God and how to please Him, he began to study the Bible daily. While driving to and from work, he listened to the New Testament on the cassette player in his car and meditated on the implications of those writings in his own life.

This executive was one of five people responsible for the programming content on his network. As the months passed, he began to question some of the values being portrayed on these shows. Many scripts that he read did not match the instructions he was reading in the Bible. Language that never used to bother him, that profaned the name of God, now caught his attention. His supervisors frequently questioned why his red pencil deleted certain sections.

One day, he received two scripts for a new situation comedy. One was about a lesbian seduction of the show's lead character. The other was about a man involved in bestiality. *These shows aren't funny,* he thought. *They're*

"I WENT OVER OUR FALL LINE-UP, J.R. ITS FULL OF SIMPLE-MINDED STORY LINES, VIOLENCE AND SEXUAL INNUENDOS, IT SHOULD BE A GREAT SEASON!"

perverse, and they don't belong on our network. His superior wanted to keep the shows with a few changes, but the man took his case to the company president, who agreed to strike the shows.

This is a true story about one man grappling with how his biblical world view affects his profession. Several times he has wanted to quit his job because of the intense pressure. Yet he is convinced that God has him where he is for a purpose and will not allow him to quit.

Television's Influence—Positive or Negative?

That man is caught in one of the main theaters of the war between the kingdoms of light and darkness. More than any other area, the media, particularly television, are shaping the thinking of our nation. According to Frederick Williams, professor of communications at the Annenberg School of Communication at the University of Southern California, "Between the ages of six and eighteen, our children will watch about 16,000 hours of TV and spend another 4,000 hours with radio, records, and movies. They will spend more time with media than with school or in talking with parents."[1] If that child attends Sunday school every week from age three, he will have 780 hours of Christian instruction from volunteer, non-professional teachers— hardly a countermeasure to the influence that television exerts.

Kevin Perrotta, author of *Taming the TV Habit*, dramatizes the real issue: "Violence and sex are not the only, or even the most serious, problems with television programming. The greater problems lie in the ways television nourishes non-Christian patterns of thinking about the world."[2]

Ask yourself: "Where did I get my attitudes toward money, leisure time, work, and my purpose in life?" Can't you see how subtle and insidious television is?

Neil Postman, professor of communications at New York University, commenting on the influence of television in our lives, has said, "Television has become what I call the command center of the culture....We go to television for everything. And the problem that results is that television, because of its entertainment format—its visual nature—turns all forms of discourse into entertainment packages."[3]

Linda and Robert Lichter and Stanley Rothman surveyed 240 journalists and broadcasters considered the most influential in the news media. These included major publications such as *The New York Times, The Washington Post, The Wall Street Journal, Time, Newsweek* and *U.S. News and World Report* plus the news departments of CBS, NBC, ABC and PBS. A second study involved 104 individuals considered "the cream of television's creative community," including presidents of independent production companies, producers, writers and network vice-presidents responsible for program development and selection.

Of the first group, 86 percent said they seldom or never attend worship services. In the second, the figure was 93 percent. Among the television leaders, 63 percent believed television should promote social reform. And what was their agenda? Ninety-seven percent believed a woman has the right to choose abortion. Seventy-five percent identified themselves as liberal politically. They feel that government should redistribute income (69 percent), that homosexuality is a valid alternate life-style (80 percent), and that extramarital affairs are acceptable (83 percent).[4]

Is it any wonder that television has become the major contributor to the moral and spiritual decadence of America?

Television producer Bill Bickley is not so concerned about the wrong that characters do in television shows as he is about a deeper issue: "Characters in the Bible did things wrong. It's that they [television characters] are portrayed with no particular code of morality. For example, instances of homosexuality are presented as something to be taken for granted rather than as a moral choice. That's what worries me most about television—not that the characters make bad choices, but that they never wrestle with moral questions."[5]

Battle Lines Are Drawn

The battle lines are clearly drawn. Television producer Norman Lear ("All in the Family" and "Mary Hartman, Mary Hartman") has formed People for the American Way to combat what he feels are attempts by some to "Christianize America."

People for the American Way was allegedly designed to emphasize "the American way," that is, "the diversity, pluralism and open democracy . . . in an atmosphere of tolerance and mutual respect"[6] that should characterize our country. By "appealing to the best instincts in people, not their fears and anxieties," People for the American Way maintains that it wishes to carry out its stated agenda.

In practice, the movement is singularly antagonistic to the expression of religious values in any public forum, and yet it promotes non-Christian values quite religiously. Even the stated attempt to appeal to "the best" in people has descended to emotional terms and propagandizing. Use of phrases such as "censorship," "ultra-right-wing" groups and "religious extremists" seeks only to appeal, in a simplistic way, to emotions, not to the intellect of potential supporters.

Yet it is obvious from the above surveys that those, such as Norman Lear, who shape the media do not reflect the beliefs of the general populace.

Fighting Back

To counteract the extremely powerful influence of the media, the nation needs more Christians like that network executive who are willing to apply a biblical world view to their profession. We need men and women who are willing to challenge the corrupt values portrayed as normal and require reporters and entertainers to begin to reflect accurately the Judeo-Christian values held dear by most Americans. In light of these goals, we propose the following:

1. Every person needs to learn to analyze and evaluate what he or she reads and views from the perspective of a biblical world view.

2. Young people who are making decisions about their careers should prayerfully consider the mass media.

We need more young Christian men and women who are highly skilled in their fields to take their places as reporters, television announcers, writers, and producers.

It is noteworthy that many journalism schools are adding ethics courses to their curricula in light of the widespread concern about the credibility of the press. Christians need to be pioneers in this area of journalistic interest.

Professor Richard Cunningham teaches a seminar in journalism ethics at New York University. He says that "journalists need an individual set of values before they enter a newsroom," and "those who don't will accumulate them as I did, by 'osmosis' over twenty-five years on the job."[7] We are concerned about the values obtained by osmosis, and we encourage Christians to conscientiously develop a biblical set of values that will direct their journalism careers from the beginning.

3. We need to consider advertiser boycotts for those companies that insist on continually sponsoring programs that ridicule Judeo-Christian values.

Rarely do we ever see a minister on secular television

portrayed in a sympathetic light, or a businessman portrayed as a responible, law-abiding citizen. Why is alcohol
consumed forty-four times for every time we see milk on
television? Why is water consumed once for every forty-
eight times alcohol is consumed? These are not pictures
of reality, and we need to pressure advertisers to support
shows that reflect our nation's real values.

Producer Bickley suggests that letters and boycotts
can be an effective means for influencing programming.

> The entire industry is based on making money. If anything
> interrupts the flow of money, it affects the industry. When com-
> panies find their advertising is having a negative effect on prod-
> uct sales, they respond. And anytime television has an economic
> problem, whether with low ratings, disgruntled advertisers, or
> controversy splitting viewing audiences, they respond. The only
> way for the public to get responses from or affect any change in
> the entertainment industry is to hit it in the money belt.[8]

Don Wildmon, a Methodist minister, is doing an effective job as executive director of the National Federation
for Decency (NFD), and he and his staff are seeing results.
ABC's "Thorn Birds" mini-series—about a Catholic priest
who broke his vow of chastity—lost six million dollars in
potential advertising revenue due to an NFD petition
campaign in 1983. Companies such as Campbell's Soup,
Ralston-Purina, and Beecham Products have redirected
their sponsorship based on input from NFD. NBC can-
celed a blatantly anti-Christian skit on "Saturday Night
Live" following letters of protest from the organization.

NFD has become a watchdog for many of us, monitoring all network prime-time TV shows, keeping accurate
records of all products and companies that advertise on
network television, and informing nearly 180,000
churches of their findings. We need to get behind such
projects, supporting the television shows that uphold
Christian values, and putting appropriate pressure on
networks and advertisers who consistently refuse to reflect those values. We need fair, objective programming.[9]

John Jones is the fourth generation of a newspaper
family. A graduate of the Columbia University Graduate
School of Journalism, he spent ten years full-time in jour-

nalism, first as a reporter, then as editor of the Greenville, Tennessee *Sun*. He recently served as the director of communications for Campus Crusade for Christ at Arrowhead Springs. Jones emphasizes the difference between "straight news reporting" and "commentary." "Straight news reporting should be characterized by fairness, objectivity and impartiality in all aspects," he says. "Commentary is designed for personal beliefs, advocacy positions, and subjective interpretation of events. Each has its own place, and its own set of rules and expectations."[10]

The problem today is that much news reporting is actually disguised commentary. There needs to be clear delineation between the two. Moreover, those who lead the news media need to realize that, all things being equal, a Christian's perspective on issues within his field of knowledge or experience is as worthy of consideration in the marketplace of ideas as the perspectives of non-Christians.

Regarding those who are Christians in journalism, Jones makes the following points:

> First and foremost, this person must excel at his job. He must be credible, honest, balanced, honorable, impartial, sensitive, and loving, and must demonstrate excellence and perception in his work.
>
> Second, he must look for legitimate story opportunities that are constructive, that give attention to things and people that are laudable, encouraging, that give a positive view of things without majoring on disaster, crime and violence.
>
> Third, a Christian can influence the media by working toward balance and fairness in reporting in contrast to what is perceived to be an imbalance against Judeo-Christian values. Often there is an unconscious, philosophical censorship of ideas simply because they are religious. Balance would suggest that all viewpoints, including those of religious people, should be included in the pursuit of a story.

There is no question that what Jones proposes is feasible. Pat Robertson is presenting a Christian world view through the Christian Broadcasting Network, which is the second largest satellite-to-cable network in the nation. The viewing audience is estimated at thirty million. The program's national "Operation Blessing" helped provide food and clothing to more than 8.5 million needy Americans in 1985.[11]

As Christians, we must do all we can to insist that the existing news and entertainment institutions provide a balanced reflection of our society, not a portrayal that reflects only the views of those who scorn Judeo-Christian values. Currently, secular humanistic values seem to dominate.

4. We need to identify, develop and network Christians who are already part of the "media influencers."

First, these men and women need to be "discovered." So often they are closet Christians because of fear of ridicule and ostracism. Not long ago, we sponsored a meeting in Manhattan with seventy Christians in responsible media positions, and a second meeting in Hollywood with some fifty others. The most common response was surprise that there were other Christians in the media.

Second, we must develop these Christian leaders spiritually. There is an urgent need for committed, spiritually reproductive believers. We must help these people understand the power of the Holy Spirit within them and train them to share their faith and be salt and light for the cause of Christ in their spheres of influence.

Almost forty years ago Bill and Vonette helped start the Hollywood Christian Fellowship. Under the leadership of Dr. Henrietta Mears, well-known personalities from the entertainment media were encouraged to receive Christ and serve Him. Among the most prominent and fruitful for God who helped to give leadership were Roy Rogers and Dale Evans. Their influence for Christ continues strong to this day.

Recently, in meeting with two new Christians in Hollywood, Ron urged a well-known actor and actress to stick it out in Hollywood to help influence their friends. Though the decadence and superficiality of Hollywood were becoming increasingly distasteful to this couple, Ron explained the need for "lighthouses" in the media. He is presently working with that couple to put together some evangelistic dinner parties in Hollywood to introduce their friends to Christ. In the meantime, he is ministering to this couple personally by telephone, books, tapes and face-to-face meetings.

Finally, Christians in media must "network" these people. They need to be put together with other Christians for encouragement and growth and to create strategies to make an impact for Christ in their spheres of influence.

That type of thing needs to happen nationally and locally—not only in the media realm, but also in every area of society. We will not elaborate on this strategy in each chapter, but it is foundational, for changes in institutions come predominantly from changed people. Though we should seek to influence the moral direction of every area of life, we must not focus our efforts on the institution alone. We must also help to change individual lives through the power of God. Then the change in the institution will be deep and pervasive, not just temporary and superficial.

Humanistic View	Biblical View
1. The media should present and advocate primarily relativistic, man-centered values	The media should at least give balanced, fair attention to Judeo-Christian values and presentations that encourage sound character
2. "Newsworthy" is strictly or predominantly defined as the criminal, tragic, bizarre, or threatening	News and entertainment should have a positive, edifying nature as much as possible
3. In entertainment programs, characters who are amoral or immoral, selfish, materialistic, and scornful of Judeo-Christian values are emphasized and sometimes glorified	At least a balance of role models should be provided to include positive presentations of those with Judeo-Christian values
4. Those in authority are consistently caricatured, made fun of, and questioned	Respect should be encouraged for properly constituted structures of authority and

those who honorably serve
in them

In this comparison chart, the points listed in the humanistic
view column are perspectives that persons from a humanist position have expressed. We do not mean to imply that every person
claiming to be a humanist would hold to every statement listed.

ACTION STEP

Evaluate your television or newpaper this week on
a daily basis, in light of the above world views. What are
your findings? What can you do to make a difference?

13

BUSINESS:

A Change Agent

How does our faith relate to business? A number of businessmen in Atlanta, Georgia, never heard the subject broached in their churches. They decided to start Fellowship of Companies for Christ (FCC), a collection of privately owned companies whose owners wanted to do a better job of integrating their faith with their business.

Bruce Wilkinson, founder and president of Walk Through the Bible, helped put FCC together. He explains: "A Christian company isn't necessarily better than a non-Christian company, but it should be different in its purpose. The members of FCC are committed to using their businesses as a platform for ministry. We have three goals in addition to making a profit: One is the salvation of our employees as well as others in our sphere of influence; two, the spiritual growth of these people; and three, service to our community. We try to get members to take part of their tithe, part of their time, and some of their company profits to help accomplish these goals."[1]

The Fellowship now has more than 250 member companies, and similar organizations have arisen around the country. Periodically they sponsor conferences in which speakers teach biblical principles on finances, leadership, goal setting, and management. "Most Christian businessmen have lost the idea that our work is our platform for ministry," says Wilkinson. "Often the ones who are known for their verbal testimony stand out negatively. They may pay their employees poorly, or simply run a poor shop. Christianity should include excellence in business as well as a verbal witness."

Does God have something to say to business people? We offer these principles for consideration:

1. Give generously to your employees.

Employers have a responsibility to God for their employees. One of the major reasons unions developed was that employers took advantage of their workers by failing to provide safe working conditions and a fair wage.

Delta Airlines is one company that is known for the way it cares for its employees and, as a result, it faced its most recent strike back in 1942. Its philosophy begins at the top with an open-door policy that allows any employee access to the chairman, president, vice-president and other top management. Input from employees is carefully considered. For instance, a committee of flight attendants chooses uniforms for Delta's 6,000 stewardesses and stewards. "That's important. You have to live in them," said one flight attendant. Mechanics even choose their immediate supervisor.[2] Delta employees were so appreciative of management that they took up a collection for a new plane and gave it to the company.

In contrast, Bill remembers using another airline whose employees were often inefficient, unfriendly, and filled with tension. Based on his observations and conversations with two or three employees, it appeared to Bill that there was almost a deliberate plan to destroy the company. "On almost every one of my flights a piece of baggage was either lost, torn, or had a grease smear on it." Bill recalls. "This airline went bankrupt.

"One day I was seated on a flight next to the vice-president of Delta Airlines. I told him how impressed I was with the cheerful, considerate, and efficient service of Delta. I also asked why the other airline had had such a hard time and had gone bankrupt. His answer was just two words: 'Disgruntled employees.'"

Christian employers and employees would do well to display the same attitude as Delta Airlines.

Looking after your employees does not mean that you overlook poor work, but it does change your approach. John Boyer, president and chairman of the board of Philadelphia Suburban Corporation, explains how his biblical world view has changed this area of his life: "I used to be very judgmental. I've had to learn to reach out in compassion and love and tell someone how he has failed, and how to learn from that. Everyone has the right to make a mistake."[3]

Those of us who are Christians should lead the way in esteeming people as very important. For we believe that every person is created in the image of God. That means that every person should be treated with respect. We, above all others, are to reflect Christ's love and compassion. It is a love that is expressed in the second great commandment, "Love your neighbor as yourself," and the Golden Rule, "Do unto others as you would have them do unto you."[4]

The late J.C. Penney adopted the Golden Rule when he started his department stores, and as a result his company has been known as the "Golden Rule Store."

Our love for one another as Christians is to be our distinguishing mark.[5] We sorely need to exhibit love toward fellow Christians first. Then we need to demonstrate Christ's love to non-Christians, especially those with whom we work or who are employed by us.

The New Testament, especially the letters of Paul, is replete with instructions on how to live out our Christian love. One excellent passage is found in Paul's letter to the Philippian church (2:3,4): "Do nothing from selfishness or empty conceit, but with humility of mind let each of you regard one another as more important than himself; do not merely look out for your own personal interests, but also for the interests of others."

Think about those people around you. Do you treat them with respect? Do you regard them as important—not just people to do a job or to fulfill a responsibility, but

important because of who they are as individuals as well
as for what they can do? Do you have their best interest
at heart? Are you concerned about their families, or does
your concern stop once they leave the work place?

Those are terribly important distinctions. Too often
we act in an un-Christian manner toward those around
us. We abuse, offend, ignore or just use people. God hates
that! People are precious. We must treat them accord-
ingly.

John Couch, past executive vice-president of a major
computer company and a close friend of ours, tells of his
experiences in the early days of the company. He ascribes
the company's meteoric growth, in great part, to the prevailing mindset of the leadership concerning the importance of people.

Once, one of his associates went through a tragic
divorce and was quite depressed. John saw the situation,
and after doing some research, he discovered that his
friend drove forty minutes one way back to his old home
daily, and that the memories there were devastating him.

So John called his friend aside and rented an apart-
ment close to the office for him so he would not have such
a long drive and such negatively reinforced memories.
He provided this as a bonus for the man. Also, various
staff invited him over regularly for meals to ease the pain
of transition.

Now that is devotion; that is love in action. And, that
ought to typify a Christian's business life-style.

2. Graciously serve your customers.

Chuck Stair is a group president of Service Master
Industries, which offers a range of services (plant management, housekeeping, laundry, food services) for health
care, educational, residential and industrial clients. This
business has grown from a $3.5 million company in 1962
to an enterprise that grossed more than $950 million in
1985. One of the company's mottos is "The cleaning people
who care." As Mr. Stair explains, "We've always looked
at our business as an instrument to help people become
all that God intended them to be. Our corporate goals are
to honor God in all we do, help people develop, pursue

excellence, and grow profitably. The first two goals are the end goals; the last two are the means. We work joyfully and very hard to serve people."[6]

It is important to note that many of the popular and bestselling books on leadership today emphasize "servant leadership." Some examples are: *In Search of Excellence; A Passion for Excellence; The One-Minute Manager; Leadership and the One-Minute Manager;* and *Intrapeneuring.* In fact, Robert K. Greenleaf of AT&T wrote an entire book, entitled *Servant Leadership: A Journey Into the Nature of Legitimate Power and Greatness.*

What is confirming in all of this is that the secular bestsellers are documenting a biblical truth—we are to lead by serving.

When Jesus was being questioned one day by his disciples who were vying for a position of authority, He responded:

> You know that the rulers of the Gentiles lord it over them, and their great men exercise authority over them. It is not so among you, but whoever wishes to become great among you shall be your servant, and whoever wishes to be first among you shall be your slave; just as the Son of Man did not come to be served, but to serve, and to give His life a ransom for many (Matthew 20:25-28).

Now reflect on that passage. Think of the implications concerning how you treat your own associates and your customers.

We *serve*—we don't bully, denigrate, push, ignore, manipulate, offend. We serve—we find needs and meet them.

Clearly, in business this means Christians should service the customer in every way possible. Obviously, we should provide the product or service we offer in an excellent way.

We did some research on customer service in our local community recently and uncovered an orthodontist who took this concept seriously. He wanted business and showed it by his actions.

The atmosphere of his office was warm and friendly. He provided books and toys for children. He sent flowers to the mothers on Mother's Day, and he put braces on the small children's Cabbage Patch dolls. That's right! He knew his clients and he served them.

Less obvious is the way we can serve our customers spiritually. We can pray for them, ask about any needs, listen to them and even, in appropriate settings, share our testimonies and the gospel.

Now, if the greatest need man has is to know God personally, how better could we serve a client than to share with him the most wonderful news ever announced? We must be sensitive, but too often we use "sensitivity" as an excuse for yielding to our fears.

Remember, God has given you a position of influence—use it.

Art DeMoss considered every business appointment a "divine appointment." He prayed daily for multitudes of people, and he shared his faith constantly. Today, some years after the death of this great man and friend of ours, his impact continues. Not only did he build a great company that served; but, more important, he used his company as a platform for touching lives for Christ.

If you don't share this truth, who will?

3. Conduct all your business with integrity.

It is often said that you cannot be successful in business unless you cheat someone, produce an inferior product, pay less than fair wages, or manipulate crooked deals. In fact, the contrary is true. Long-range success depends upon reliability, integrity, authenticity, honesty, and priority consideration for employees and customers alike.

One of the benefits of the presidency of Ronald Reagan has been partial deregulation of industry. Implied in such loosening of restrictions is responsibility. Businessmen ought to consider regulating themselves. More groups like Fellowship of Companies for Christ should be started throughout the nation so that businessmen gather to study how the Bible applies to business, and then hold each other accountable to be ethical and honorable in all of their dealings.

Chris White saw a change in his attitude after he met Christ at age thirty-six. "I was a very aggressive, competitive person," he says. "But I began acting graciously. For example, a sales manager of an adjacent territory disputed one of my accounts. It was not clear to whose territory it belonged. Earlier, before meeting Christ, I would have fiercely fought for the account. Now, the Holy Spirit empowered me to reflect God's benevolent character of graciousness which was revealed to Moses in Exodus 34:6.[7] Instead, I gave my opponent the benefit of the doubt. This was God's way of handling the situation, not Chris White's."[8]

Some may be called to leave their jobs when their biblical world view cannot be reconciled to the job. Others have been able to incorporate their world view into their work. John Boyer says, "When we get into problems, I've got a Bible in my office and we refer to it often. You make many decisions where the only person you have to advise you is the Holy Spirit."[9]

We would like to see that become the desire of every Christian businessman. Chuck Stair put it well: "When we as Christian leaders want to bring out the best in our people, we have the responsibility of helping them *grow* as individuals so that they in turn grow in their ability to handle their responsibilities...thereby improving their level of contribution. This is as much our 'mission' as any tangible goal of our Christian organizations."[10]

4. Beware of becoming calloused or greedy.

We are privileged and particularly blessed that we live in a country that acknowledges the value of private ownership of property. Our country's economic system, the free enterprise system, has allowed us to be blessed materially beyond measure compared with any other nation in history.

But, there is need for a word of caution. Paul warned his young disciple, Timothy, of the danger of loving money. He says, "Those who want to get rich fall into temptation and a snare and many foolish and harmful desires which plunge men into ruin and destruction. For the love of money is a root of all sorts of evil, and some by longing for it have wandered away from the faith, and pierced themselves with many a pang" (1 Timothy 6:9,10).

Our free enterprise system allows for more personal freedom than other economic systems. Not only is there greater freedom to be responsible and demonstrate charitable love; there is also the freedom to be irresponsible, dishonest, and greedy. The inherent weakness is not in this economic system but in the nature of man. We must wear the cloak of materialism loosely. Further, we must be careful as a nation that we do not view our salvation as consisting of our economy and economic system. Instead, we should view every area of life, including our economic system, as an opportunity to demonstrate responsible stewardship, quality work, honesty, and charity before God, who owns all things.

Money in and of itself is not evil. It is a medium of exchange. But the insatiable desire for more and more money is dangerous. If we follow the tendency to trust riches rather than God, we fail to acknowledge the real source from which all blessings come. No matter how much God blesses us, it all belongs to Him and we are His stewards.

Paul, in Ephesians 4:28, gives us the reason for increasing our riches through our labors. "But rather let him labor, performing with his own hands what is good, in order that he may have something to share with him who has a need." Notice "*in order* that he may have something *to share* with him who has a need." God wants us

"I LOVE MY CREDIT CARDS. I PAY OFF MASTERCARD WITH VISA, VISA WITH CITIBANK, CITIBANK WITH AMERICAN EXPRESS, AMERICAN EXPRESS WITH..."

to be His wealth distributors. Blessing comes from giving, not getting.[11]

Another word of caution is warranted. We need to give with discretion and discernment. We are to be wise as serpents and harmless as doves. That means that we do not, through our undiscerning giving, contribute to the ongoing irresponsibility of some of those who ask for help. For example, it would not be loving to give a beggar money he requests for food in order for him to go and spend it for alcohol. Instead, offer to take him to a coffee shop and buy him a sandwich. Do you know for what your gifts of money are used? We as Christians are to be wise in our giving!

As you give, certainly remember those who have physical needs. But remember, the greatest need man has is the need to know God. Give faithfully to your church. Research those institutions that most effectively reach the lost for Christ and build them into His likeness, then support them generously.

Also, do not give only your money. Your time and talents are resources, too. Do not become calloused, and do not be greedy. Give yourself away.

In addition to inculcating biblical principles in our lives and spheres of influence, we should also "walk our talk." We need to press on to identify and develop Christian executives at a national and local level and help them "network" with one another. This has been amplified further in chapter 12.

Furthermore, executives need to see their positions as a platform from which to expose people to the claims of Christ. Throughout America today, men and women are involved in executive dinner parties, retreats, conferences and other ministries aimed at winning people to Christ.

Clad in well-tailored business attire, P.S. Freburg has the appearance of a professional woman, dressed for success. At noon you might find her seated in velvet-covered chairs at Denver's Petroleum Club, leading a Bible study or discipleship group. This is in stark contrast to her surroundings at breakfast. That morning she could be found among drunks, derelicts and street people, pouring coffee with a nondenominational group seeking to help feed the homeless. In addition to her support of Christian works, she is also assisting, financially and personally, in establishing a shelter during the day where the homeless can relax and converse. These conversations regularly turn to spiritual matters, with many accepting the good news of the gospel. Beyond her financial backing, P.S. purchased the paint and other renovation supplies and even took up the paintbrush herself. Her response to questions about her involvement: "It's not that I'm the one doing it, but that God is doing it through me. Frankly, it's not that I always want to minister, but it sometimes is a case of dying to self and persevering on to do what God wants me to do."[12]

The point is that we are here to "seek first God's kingdom and His righteousness."[13] Therefore, our occupation ought to be maximized to achieve these ends.

Humanistic View	Biblical View
1. Make a name for myself	Do all to the glory of God, and not for myself
2. God helps those who help themselves	God helps those who are dependent on Him and take the initiative to trust and obey Him in the power of the Holy Spirit
3. Make lots of money for my own pleasure	Don't lay up treasures on earth, but be a good steward in expanding God's kingdom
4. It's a dog-eat-dog world out there, so I must use every method available to succeed	Do all to the glory of God, and don't yield to expediency
5. My job is my most important priority	Godly character in myself and in my family is paramount

In this comparison chart, the points listed in the humanistic view column are perspectives that persons from a humanist position have expressed. We do not mean to imply that every person claiming to be a humanist would hold to every statement listed.

ACTION STEP

List three specific steps you can take to demonstrate an improved biblical approach to your business.

Step 1 _____

_____

_____

Step 2 _____

_____

_____

Step 3 _____

_____

_____

TEN COMMANDMENTS FOR BUSINESS

Lt. Col. Nimrod McNair, Jr., (USAF ret.) has developed the following principles for businessmen, based on scriptural truths, and teaches them in seminars as part of his involvement with Campus Crusade for Christ's Executive Ministry.

1. Show proper respect for authority.
2. Maintain a singleness of purpose.
3. Use effective communication.
4. Provide rest and recreation.
5. Counsel with the elders.
6. Show proper respect for human dignity.
7. Maintain a stability of the sexes.
8. Demonstrate the proper allocation of resources.
9. Demonstrate honesty and integrity.
10. Maintain the right of ownership of property.

14

GOVERNMENT:

A God-ordained Tool

"**I**n order to ensure to citizens freedom of conscience, the church...is separated from the state, and the school from the church."

Is that statement a part of the United States Constitution? In a survey conducted by the Gallup Organization shortly before the 1984 presidential election, 45 percent of all Americans believed this was taken from their Constitution.[1]

In fact, *it is a direct quote from the Constitution of the Soviet Union.*

The following is what the First Amendment to the United States Constitution actually says: "Congress shall make no law respecting an establishment of religion, or prohibiting the free exercise thereof; or abridging the freedom of speech or of the press; or the right of the people peaceably to assemble, and to petition the government for a redress of grievances."

In no way does this wording imply that government and religious faith are totally separated. In fact, participation in government by people of all faiths is encouraged. The First Amendment was written in order to prevent what happened in England and a number of European countries, where a particular religion or denomination became the official state religion and was so intertwined with civil government that anyone outside that belief had difficulty participating in the governmental process.

Because of the way the United States government is structured as a constitutional republic, we believe that all Christians have a responsibility to be involved in the process of government. Not to do so is to be a poor steward before God of the blessings that He has given to us as individuals and as a nation. We believe that in the marketplace of ideas, the biblical world view needs to be strongly stated and matched against other world views. That is our right and our biblical responsibility under the Constitution. Unfortunately, many would deny Christians that right.

We often hear the statement, "You can't legislate morality." In fact, every piece of legislation is a moral statement. Our question is, "What is the foundation by which moral judgments are made to formulate legislation?" Thomas Jefferson wrote, "Can the liberties of a nation be thought secure, when we have removed their only firm basis, a conviction in the minds of the people that these liberties are the gifts of God?"[2]

Harold O.J. Brown wrote in *The Reconstruction of the Republic:*

> The United States Constitution is not a source of fundamental values. It is an instrument whereby fundamental values can be protected, defining the procedures, principles, and methods whereby government can function to allow the people to give content to their lives. But the Constitution itself cannot give that content. In the early days, no one supposed that it would. There was a sufficiently clear value-consensus among Americans so that, while degrees of commitment or differences existed, there was little doubt as to the fundamental nature of good and evil, of virtue and vice. These things were not defined in the Constitution because Americans of the federal era generally knew and agreed about what they are. Today, if there is disagreement or ignorance—as increasingly there is—fundamental values cannot be found in the Constitution. They simply are not there.[3]

Recognizing the Need for Religious Values

Today increasingly more non-Christians realize our nation's need for religious values. The Brookings Institute, generally perceived as liberal in its appraisals, views and recommendations, said in a 1986 report entitled "Religion in American Public Life," that without religion "democracy lacks essential moral support" to sustain it. The report concluded that secular value systems fail to do the job of holding a society together. Representative government, the report said, "depends for its health on values that over the not-so-long run must come from religion." Through religion, "human rights are rooted in the moral worth with which a loving Creator has endowed each human soul, and social authority is legitimized by making it answerable to a transcendent moral law."[4]

Specifically related to the First Amendment, the report said that, "[the Amendment] is no more neutral on the general value of religion than it is on the general value of free exchange of ideas or an independent press."[5]

So where are those transcendent, fundamental values to be found? We believe they are found in the Bible. The Bible basically delineates between four levels of government, and we have examined the first three earlier in this book. First, there is self-government—each person is responsible for his or her own decisions and behavior.[6] The second is family government.[7] The third is ecclesiastical or church government.[8]

Finally, there is civil government. Just as God established the family and church as the primary social institutions, so God has established the state as His minister for civil protection and justice.[9] God has given civil government the biblical responsibilities of commending those who do right, punishing crime, preserving peace against external and internal attack, establishing a legal system based on biblical principles, and promoting an atmosphere of tranquility that permits the gospel of Christ to be freely preached and lived.[10]

It is important to understand this biblical basis of government because too often people expect the federal government to involve itself in areas that are rightfully the responsibility of other forms of government—for example, social programs such as welfare. We do not necessarily advocate doing away with all governmental social aid programs. There are many people who have legitimate needs that are beyond their ability to meet and for which they are not directly responsible. Our problem has been a growing tendency to depend on the federal or state governments to meet the needs that God has ordained individuals, families, and churches to fulfill. In the early history of our country, most of the poor were cared for by their families, churches and other private agencies. Now most churches have little incentive to minister to the poor, since that need is being "met" by government. The family and church should resume their responsibilities and encourage solutions based on private-sector initiatives. It will do little good to complain about government encroachment in this area, unless, at the same time, Christians begin to provide alternatives and fulfill their biblical responsibilities.

The problem is that most people do not stop to think through the implications of a social program, or of any other piece of legislation. Too many people believe that all problems must be solved on a civil governmental level.

" OKAY, SIR ...CAN YOU PICK OUT THE GUY WHO SHOT YOU
WHILE YOU WERE MUGGING HIM ?

Special interest groups often focus only on what would benefit them rather than on the general welfare of the nation.

Let's Get Involved Again

We believe it is essential for Christians to begin to think biblically about civil government issues. Citizens need to decide their positions based not on emotional appeal or desire, but on a thorough understanding of Scripture. In addition, we would like to propose the following steps for involvement in the government process.

1. Develop a standard for evaluating and recruiting political candidates.

Based on a biblical world view, we should evaluate every candidate and potential candidate on his or her track record of integrity, morality, and adherence to Judeo-Christian principles, in addition to relevant experience, knowledge, and demonstrated ability to handle responsibilities similar to those required by the office. That grid should determine whom we support, for whom we campaign, and for whom we vote. Just because a person is a Christian does not automatically qualify him for public office. While we would prefer a Christian, we should consider voting for a Jew, or a person of another faith, or no faith, if he demonstrates that he will take a more effective and proper biblical stand on the issues and lives a good, moral life. Too many people vote simply on their perception of a candidate as he or she is presented in the media, or on the basis of a candidate's political affiliation, rather than on carefully thought-through criteria.

2. We need to help elect candidates who have a world view that is consistent with a biblical world and life view.

Senator Bill Armstrong, who was honorary co-chairman of the National Committee for the Year of the Bible in 1983, believes the Bible has much to say about how to think about legislation. He says, "The Bible has become the greatest source by which my intellect is enlightened." He gives an example concerning the issue of national defense:

> I have thought over and over again about the book of
> Nehemiah. You remember that Nehemiah had a great heart for
> his country. He was concerned about...the collapse of the walls
> of Jerusalem. Do you remember what he did first? He prayed.
> He said, 'Lord, help me; help me to be Your servant and to do
> what needs to be done. I am concerned about the way the walls
> and the gates of Jerusalem have fallen down.' And presently his
> employer, the King of Persia, permitted him to go back to
> Jerusalem.
>
> When he got there, he did three things: He rebuilt the wall—
> that is to say, he restored the defense of the city. Second, he set
> an example of incorruptible administration....And third, he re-
> stored the religious practice. He centered the life of the city back
> on the living God.
>
> Now how does that relate to America? What do you suppose
> would happen if we would do just that? If we rebuilt our defenses
> and established a standard of incorruptible administration—and
> by that I don't mean just official corruption, but I mean leader-
> ship that is not self-seeking....And most important, if we put the
> Lord at the center of our national life?
>
> I don't want to overdraw the parallel, but I'm just drawn
> back to it over and over again as an example...of what we should
> strive for in our country.[11]

Have you ever heard of Charles Evans Hughes? He
would have been President of the United States instead
of Woodrow Wilson in 1916 if only one more voter in each
California district had voted for him.[12] In 1960, John F.
Kennedy was elected President over Richard Nixon by
less than a single vote per election precinct.[13] In that year,
just over 60 percent of all eligible citizens voted. In 1980,
that number had declined to 53.9 percent, which means
that Ronald Reagan was elected president by less than
28 percent of eligible voting Americans.[14] We can never
overestimate the power of a single vote.

Every person should be involved, at least on the precinct level, in working to elect people of moral integrity.
According to the Federal Election Commission there were
180,351 voting precincts in the United States as of the
1984 general election. If one person in each precinct
worked conscientiously to elect such candidates, we could
make a significant difference among the men and women

"THOSE LETTERS ARE IMPORTANT! THEY KEEP THE VOTERS INFORMED OF GOVERNMENT WASTE!"

who create our laws. Voting biblically is a matter of stewardship under God. "The good influence of godly citizens causes a city [state or nation] to prosper..."[15]

3. Young people need to consider making a career in government.

Morton Blackwell understands how that can happen. He was Louisiana state chairman of the College Republicans and the youngest Goldwater delegate at the Republican National Convention in 1964. In recent years, he was policy director for Senator Gordon Humphrey of New Hampshire; President Reagan's top Youth Campaign advisor; and served three years in the Reagan administration as the President's chief liaison with conservative groups.

In 1979, Blackwell founded the Leadership Institute, a non-profit, non-partisan foundation designed to give young people who are fundamentally sound philosophically the technical and organizational proficiency to help win elections and to serve on the staffs of elected officials. After the conservative landslide in 1980, Blackwell found, "There simply were not enough experienced conservative staff members to go around."[16] The result was that conservative senators and congressmen hired staff who did not share the views and goals of the member of Congress. Such a staff member, in a privileged and powerful position, who is not committed to the same platform on which the senator or congressman was elected, can do much to undermine the effectiveness of that elected representative.

Blackwell has also organized a political action committee, the Committee for Responsible Youth Politics, and has isolated basic principles for deciding which candidates to support.[17]

4. We must be involved in government on the local level.

Dr. Stephen F. Hotze was concerned when the Houston city council passed a law which amended the civil affirmative action code to include the term "sexual orientation" in addition to the non-discrimination requirements for the standard areas of race, religion, sex and the handicapped. A petition was distributed among a large contingent of pastors, and 64,000 signatures were gathered to refer the law to a general election. He also formed "Houstonians for Traditional Values" and several other political action groups to help push the cause.

While the Gay Political Caucus dominated news coverage of the issue, Dr. Hotze found that the key to success lay not with the news media. "Campaigns are won down at the grassroots level," he said, "neighbor to neighbor, block by block."[18] The hard work paid off in early 1985 when the conservative community surprised the media and won an overwhelming victory by 81 percent to 19 percent. It exposed how a small group of people, the so-called homosexual vote, had such a tremendous influence that they forced politicians to kow-tow to their petty demands. And it showed how Christians, if they assume the mandate given by Christ to take dominion, can reclaim this world for Christ.

The reason Dr. Hotze is involved in the political process is the same reason each one of us must be involved. "If we boil everything down, our view of who owns our life and property will determine what we do with our life and property. Either we and everything we have belongs to God or we have a humanistic view that accepts the state as sovereign. Whoever we believe controls us becomes our Lord. The view we adopt will inevitably decide the future of our families, our Christian liberties, and our estates."

Humanistic View	Biblical View
1. Government is sovereign	God is sovereign
2. Government grants and guarantees rights	God delegates responsibilities and establishes boundaries of protected freedoms and jurisdictional authority
3. The human government we call the state (civil government: local, regional, national) is the only one that has authority	God's government is the one that matters. He has ordained three primary social governing institutions: the family, the church and the state (civil), each having different responsibilities and spheres of authority
4. Christians shouldn't get involved in "dirty politics"	Christians are the salt and light and need to spread the influence of the gospel
5. Vote along party lines or for interest-group priorities	Vote for what best represents the biblical view
6. Christians should be involved only in church activities	Christians should make a righteous difference in all areas of life including the public affairs of their communities and nation

In this comparison chart, the points listed in the humanistic view column are perspectives that persons from a humanist position have expressed. We do not mean to imply that every person claiming to be a humanist would hold to every statement listed.

ACTION STEP

Which of the above world views reflects your thinking? Your actions?

What *one thing* can you do to have an effect on government this year?

15

LAW:

Back to Its Roots

Probate Judge Randall J. Hekman of Kent County, Michigan, faced a difficult situation. A thirteen-year-old girl, at the request of her mother, had become a neglect ward of the court. When the girl became pregnant, she requested that the court allow her to obtain an abortion because her mother had refused to give authorization. Initially, Judge Hekman ruled that he had no authority over the decision. But further study of the law convinced him that the State's Supreme Court would overturn the Michigan statute that gave a parent veto power over the supposed rights of a girl. So when the girl's attorney pressed for action, Judge Hekman was forced to make a decision.

"My initial reaction was to disqualify myself and give this hot potato to another judge," Hekman said in an interview with *Moody Monthly* magazine. But after seeking counsel, he decided that "disqualification was neither legally required nor morally right....It bothered me that I should be considered a less than adequate juvenile court judge because I could not order the killing of what I know medically to be a human, unborn living child....I believe there's a higher law of God that no man has the authority to repeal."[1]

The young girl was in the fifth month of her pregnancy when the hearing was held. Judge Hekman had little time to render his decision. His research told him, "The law would require me to disregard the rights of the unborn child and base the entire decision on the best interests of the pregnant girl. After devoting much of my opinion to the law as I interpreted it, I stated that I had a problem disregarding the rights of the unborn."[2]

Judge Hekman suggested that it was not asking too much for the mother to extend her discomfort for a few more weeks for the sake of the unborn child's right to live. His study of the Supreme Court decision in the case of *Roe vs. Wade* convinced him that the opinion did not "carry the force of law for any parties other than the actual litigants of the 1973 case itself."[3] Therefore, he refused to order the abortion. Three months later, the girl wrote him thanking him for the decision, which had caused her to do some serious thinking about the life she was carrying.

Judge Hekman's decision caused the National Organization for Women to file a complaint with the Michigan Judicial Tenure Commission, which had authority to remove him from office if he had violated ethical standards. The commission did warn him before it dismissed the charges to be careful in the future.

Upholding the law is a serious responsibility about which the Bible has much to say. "You shall not pervert justice," Moses wrote in Exodus 23:6. Later, as the Israelites were preparing to enter the promised land, he reminded the people: "Hear the cases between your fellow countrymen, and judge righteously between a man and his fellow countrymen....You shall hear the small and the great alike. You shall not fear man, for the judgment is God's. And the case that is too hard for you, you shall bring to me, and I will hear it."[4] The Bible has literally dozens of references to just and unjust judges and judgments.

U.S. Legal System Rooted in Judeo-Christian Principles

In the United States, many of us have forgotten that much of our legal system was founded on Judeo-Christian principles, the moral standards which comprised the value system of the founding fathers. As the United States became more and more of a melting pot, absorbing the

ethnic cultures and class struggles of other countries, emphasis shifted toward a more humanistic interpretation of the Constitution, under the guise of "equal access to the law." At least one organization, the American Civil Liberties Union, has helped neutralize the Judeo-Christian underpinnings of our legal system by seeking new legal precedents.

The ACLU, founded by Roger Baldwin in 1920, was originally formed to aid those who were engaged in the labor struggle. Baldwin's ideals were Marxist in origin, and he admitted that "At the bottom I am for conserving the full powers of every person on earth by expanding them to their individual limits... I am for socialism, disarmament and ultimately for abolishing the state itself as an instrument of violence and compulsion. I seek social ownership of property, the abolition of the propertied class and sole control by those who produce wealth."[5]

In pursuing "equal access" for their clients, it appears that the ACLU has allowed a kind of religious pluralism to creep across the land. Like their founder, the ACLU has argued that Judeo-Christian religious expression in public schools or on public property is tantamount to the establishment of a state religion. Why are we not countering their efforts, taking the initiative to uphold biblical values?

One way to combat this trend is for Christian lawyers to champion those who support the early foundations of our society and Judeo-Christian principles in our country's commerce. Christian lawyers themselves must go back to the original covenant relationship of the law. Even when it requires a sacrifice in finances, security and a comfortable life-style, Christian lawyers and judges can lead us back to Judeo-Christian principles with as much enthusiasm as the ACLU has shown in leading us away from them. And we need to support these individuals.

Rutherford Institute Leads An Offensive

John Whitehead is one such example. When he was graduated from law school in 1974, he admits that he was "practicing a kind of atheist agnosticism." After reading *The Late Great Planet Earth* by Hal Lindsey, he was forced to evaluate the claims of the Bible based on the fact that its prophecies were being fulfilled. After becoming a Christian, "I started re-orienting my beliefs on law and what it should be used for. I was already an activist, working with an attorney from the ACLU. I began thinking about what the law should be used for in terms of the Body of Christ."[6]

He spent a year in seminary and during that time was approached by a public school teacher who had briefly shared her faith in the classroom in answer to a student's question. She had been reprimanded by her superintendent. "At that point, I didn't know there was a problem with Christian rights. I couldn't believe that a person couldn't share his faith in a public school for two minutes.

That didn't seem right. But I remember that I was taught in law school that everything about religion in public was unconstitutional."[7]

That motivated him to start studying the law in a new light. He discovered that what he had been taught was a distortion of the truth. That led to his first book, *The Separation Illusion*, which examined the issue of church and state from a conservative, biblical viewpoint.

Today, John Whitehead directs the Rutherford Institute, an organization that might be described as a Christian counterpart to the ACLU. Their philosophy is to be a vehicle for lawyers to use their professional training to be salt and light in society. They defend their clients without fee in situations regarding Christians' legal rights to freedom of speech and practice.

James and Debbie Cooper were cleared of child abuse charges with the help of attorney James Henry, vice-president of the Rutherford Institute of Tennessee. The Chattanooga City School System had charged that the parents were "neglecting their parental responsibility and therefore aiding the deprivation of the children's education" because the Coopers' two daughters were taught at home.[8] In fact, the Coopers provided their daughters systematic instruction in such subjects as reading, math, science, social studies, art, music, computer science and Bible. A Circuit Court judge ruled in favor of the Coopers after James Henry argued successfully that the state's compulsory education law was unconstitutional.

The Rutherford Institute has aided in many similar cases and has also become a discipleship ministry, taking law students as well as practicing attorneys and involving them in an internship program that provides practical on-the-job experience. Through this, Whitehead hopes that Christian lawyers will be more aware and active in putting their faith into practice in every area of law. "Most professionals are into the money game," he says. "Jesus left this world with basically no earthly possessions. I believe we're put here to affect things, and you can't affect society only by going to church on Sunday. It has to be a total encompassing ministry from the time you awake until the time you go to bed at night."[9]

"YOU'RE BEING SUED FOR MALPRACTICE FOR LOSING A MALPRACTICE SUIT!"

A Cohesive Strategy

This, of course, is just one practical thing that can happen. But there is *much more* that should happen. For example, Christians need to support and extend the work of fine organizations like the Rutherford Institute—to identify, train and network existing Christian lawyers with the goal of influencing their communities and professions for the cause of Christ and advancing positive societal change.

Furthermore, a new corps of radically committed, Christian lawyers are needed—attorneys who will take their faith into the courtroom. Additionally, the legal profession itself needs to be re-established in the bedrock of the Word of God and God's nature as the foundation for proper legal interpretation. The sociological, relativistic approach to law is quicksand.[10]

We must regain the high ground in law.

Humanistic View	Biblical View
1. There are no absolutes; therefore, law is what the majority or judicial elite say it is	God, through His Word, is the final arbiter of truth in law
2. Don't rock the boat on moral and ethical issues	Be courageous in resisting moral and ethical compromise
3. Use the profession primarily to make a comfortable life	Resist evil, regardless of cost
4. Represent only the interests of your client	Represent God's standards

In this comparison chart, the points listed in the humanistic view column are perspectives that persons from a humanist position have expressed. We do not mean to imply that every person claiming to be a humanist would hold to every statement listed.

ACTION STEP

Do you know a lawyer who has God's view of the law and our society? Send his name to the Rutherford Institute at P.O. Box 510, Manassas, VA 22110.

16

EDUCATION:

Brainwashed or Informed?

In April of 1983, an eighteen-member panel appointed by then Education Secretary Terrel H. Bell revealed the results of a year-and-a-half-long study by the National Commission on Excellence in Education. Its report, entitled "A Nation at Risk: The Imperative for Educational Reform," stated:

> If an unfriendly foreign power had attempted to impose on America the mediocre educational performance that exists today, we might well have viewed it as an act of war.[1]

We have every reason to be outraged concerning the quality of public education in the United States. In 1910 the U.S. Bureau of Education stated that public schools would "in a short time practically eliminate illiteracy."[2] Today, according to Department of Education statistics, there are "24 million functional illiterates in the United States, virtually all of whom have had from eight to twelve years of compulsory public schooling," says historian and educator, Samuel Blumenfeld.[3] *Time* magazine reports that 13 percent of all seventeen-year-olds are functionally illiterate.[4]

By almost any means of evaluation, our system of public education is in trouble. As "A Nation at Risk" states:

> Each generation of Americans has outstripped its parents in education, in literacy and in economic attainment.
>
> For the first time in the history of our country, the educational skills of one generation will not surpass, will not equal, will not even approach, those of their parents.

The report concluded that "our very future as a Nation and a people" are at stake.[5]

It is impossible to address so large a concern in the space of such a few pages. However, we hope to stimulate you to think about the problem and take action. We propose at least five ways people can become involved in reforming the ideas that drive our system of education.

FLASH: THE SUPREME COURT REMOVED D, G, AND O FROM THE ALPHABET BECAUSE WHEN ARRANGED IN A CERTAIN WAY THEY FOSTER RELIGION.

A Call to Action: What Is the Purpose of Education?

1. All we do in education must be done in light of its purpose.

Much of what happens concerning our schools goes unquestioned because we have forgotten the roots of public education. In fact, it was not until the mid-1800s that government at the local and state levels began assuming a major role. The first public schools, called common schools, were created in New England as a means of communicating Calvinist Puritan religion from one generation to the next. Greek, Latin, and Hebrew were taught to aid students in their study of Scripture. Harvard College (later University) was founded in 1636, with the aid of government funds, as a seminary for educating the commonwealth's future Christian leaders.[6]

Horace Mann is generally considered the father of modern education, for he is the one who diligently worked in his position as secretary of the Board of Education in Massachusetts in the 1830s and '40s to organize a centralized, state-controlled school system financed by taxes on property. But it was primarily the ideas of British social reformer Robert Owen that influenced Mann. Owen wrote extensively about the transformation of society, to make it free from what he saw as the restricting influence of religion. The following is a sample, written by Owen in the August 4, 1832, *Free Enquirer*:

> Do ye ask me wherein I put my trust, if religious responsibilities are annihilated? In human goodness. Do ye enquire what I propose as a substitute for religion? Cultivation of the noble faculties of the human mind....
>
> Let us train children to integrity, and we shall have honest men and women....Let us give children facts for spiritualities, good habits for long sermons, the truths of science for the mysteries of creeds, kindness for fear, and liberality for sectarianism....I would as little prejudice a child against any religion as in its favor; I would not speak to it on the subject. It should learn first what it could see and understand: its judgment should be carefully matured, and its reasoning powers sedulously cultivated.[7]

That philosophy pervades education today. The National Education Association, ostensibly a labor union for public school teachers, is a powerful lobby that zealously advocates the liberal view of education. "It is virtually a political party," claims Blumenfeld. "From my study of NEA resolutions, it is obvious that it is aiming for a total educational dictatorship under which it will be impossible for anyone to teach anybody anything in this country without a license from the NEA."[8]

The NEA goals, reflecting its world view, are clearly stated:

> ...the goal of education must be to develop individuals who are open to change...to develop a society in which people can live more comfortably with change than with rigidity. In the

coming world the capacity to face the new appropriately is more important than the ability to know and repeat the old.[9]

...this view of humankind requires the educative process to free people to be themselves. It values autonomy...and interdependence....The imposition of constraints and conventions...can retard the individual's growth.[10]

Why do we educate our children? We need to answer that question in light of our world view. The Bible has much to say about that, including our second principle.

Whose Responsibility To Educate?

2. Education is ultimately the responsibility of parents, not the state.

The basic center of learning should be the home, not the school. The church and school should be extensions of the home and the parents. Moses commanded the Israelites to teach the commands of God "diligently unto thy children."[11] The writer of Proverbs says to parents, "Train up a child in the way he should go."[12] The psalmist wrote, "The fear of the Lord is the beginning of wisdom."[13] We could refer to many scriptural passages that demonstrate how God has given the responsibility of education to parents and that education is not simply intellectual, but requires us to teach our children the ways of God.

If that is true, then we are abdicating our responsibility and authority when we simply send our children to school—public or private—without providing any further input. Parents need to be active in the education of their children. This goes far beyond sending them to a Christian school. This can help, but it does not replace the personal responsibility of the mother, and particularly, the father.[14] At the very least, parents need to talk with their children about what they are learning in school. In addition, they should communicate frequently with the children's teachers and school administrators, in order to understand what is being taught and the purpose behind that teaching. Many teachers welcome parents as teacher's aides in their classrooms.

We believe Christian parents should be active in their local school associations and knowledgeable about every aspect of their children's schools. If so led, they should run for the local school board and actively work to influence their educational system.

Many parents today are "home schooling." In this approach the parents fully educate their children at home for a period of time.[15] In fact, Ron and his wife, Mary, have "home schooled" their children, Matt and Molly, for a couple of years of their education. They have found this to be rewarding, highly gratifying, and effective for children and parents alike.

What Is the Foundation of Education?

3. Parents and teachers should actively work to see that a biblical world view is the foundation of education.

Steve Wyper teaches World Civilization and United States History at Arlington High School in Riverside, California. He admits what many educators refuse to admit, that "I cannot separate my total beliefs from what I am doing," though he does not force his beliefs on his students.[16]

His approach is to teach contrasting beliefs side by side so that students can make intelligent decisions about what they believe. He teaches creation and evolution and comparative religions in this manner, helping his students to evaluate underlying presuppositions. "For example, one statement in our textbook said that we can't learn much about Jesus because there's no reliable historical information. Since it's in the book, most students would readily accept it. I took that statement and showed them the problem with it by presenting some evidence."

Wyper's methods have had interesting repercussions. Once after a class in which he had discussed chemical dating methods, some of his students went to biology class where the instructor began saying, "This fossil has been dated as three million years old." Several students challenged that assumption, and the teacher in turn challenged Wyper. That led to a three-year debate, and eventually the biology teacher committed his life to Christ.

Contrary to popular belief, it is *not* illegal for teachers or students to talk about their faith in the classroom. Constitutional lawyer John W. Whitehead has addressed this:

> The First Amendment, as interpreted and defined by the United States Supreme Court, means that the government has no authority to restrict expression because of "its message, its ideas, its subject matter, or its content." (*Police Department of Chicago v. Mosley*, 408 U.S. 92, 95 (1972).) As the Court has said: "It is the purpose of the First Amendment to preserve an uninhibited marketplace of ideas in which truth will ultimately prevail, rather than to countenance monopolization of that market, whether it be by the government itself or a private licensee." (*Red Lion Broadcasting Company v. Federal Communication Commission*, 395 U.S. 367, 390 (1969).)[17]

The Supreme Court also ruled in the case of *Tinker v. Des Moines Independent School District*: "It can hardly be argued that either students or teachers shed their constitutional rights...at the schoolhouse gate."[18]

Steve Wyper has some practical advice for Christian teachers. First, live your faith realistically in the classroom and among your peers. Second, learn your subject well, not just the facts, but the underlying presuppositions so that you can deal with Christian truth in the context of your teaching. Third, remember that man is created in the image of God, therefore each person in your classroom is special. Finally, don't preach, but be prepared to lead people to Christ when the opportunity presents itself.

Teachers Are Examples

4. Teachers need to use their influence as examples of a godly life-style.
Ann Landers printed a letter from a school teacher that emphasizes the influence of a teacher in the life of a student:

> I have come to a frightening conclusion that I am the decisive element in the classroom. It is my personal approach that creates the climate. It is my daily mood that makes the weather. As a teacher I possess a tremendous power to make a child's life miserable or joyous. I can be a tool of torture or an instrument of inspiration. I can humiliate or humor, hurt or heal. In all situations it is my response that decides whether the crisis will be escalated or deescalated and a child humanized or dehumanized.[19]

Sometimes a biblical world view and a godly life-style can be costly. Biblically based convictions may lead to actions that could cost you your job. In any battle, there are wounds, but God will be faithful no matter what the outcome. Steve Wyper took such a stand when he refused to support a teachers' strike: "I refused to strike on the basis of biblical principles. I did not have the right to tell my employer what to pay me. My reason for being a teacher was not determined by salary. Naturally, I want a bigger salary like everyone else. But, striking was not going to help my teaching of the kids, and that was my primary function."

Steve is doing what we all should do, whatever our profession: model ourselves after biblical principles, look for opportunities to win people to Christ, speak out on issues, and work for fundamental moral change.

Educational Reform

5. We need to work to reform higher education.
The reason for many of the problems in elementary and secondary education relates to the fact that most teachers go through a training program that is permeated with humanistic philosophy. Steven Muller, president of

Johns Hopkins University in Baltimore, is concerned about that problem:

> The biggest failing in higher education today is that we fall short in exposing students to values....This situation has come about because the modern university is rooted in the scientific method, having essentially turned its back on religion. I'm not hostile to the scientific method—it is a marvelous means of inquiry, and it has been highly productive—but it really doesn't provide a value system.[20]

"WE'RE NOT INSTILLING GOOD CHARACTER TRAITS IN KIDS?! BUT WE GOT RID OF EVERYTHING THAT WOULD HURT THEIR LITTLE MINDS... PRAYER, CREATION SCIENCE AND BIBLE STUDIES!"

That is precisely why we have begun the International Christian Graduate University. There are many fine Christian colleges, but very few graduate programs that allow students to prepare from a biblical world view perspective for professions like medicine, law, and media communications. Our dream is that this university might be a vehicle to inspire millions of men and women to go into these professions and help restore them to the moral foundation on which they were started.

Here too we must identify, develop, and "network" the key Christian leaders in order to influence this sphere of activity, both locally and nationally, for the cause of Christ and societal change.

Humanistic View	Biblical View
1. Education is the state's responsibility	Education is the parents' responsibility
2. Educational choices belong to the state	Educational choices belong to the parents
3. The goal is to make good citizens	The goal is godly character and biblical thinkers
4. The teacher is a change agent to spread secular values	The teacher is a model of godly character and parental values
5. Education is the way of salvation	Education begins with the fear of the Lord

In this comparison chart, the points listed in the humanistic view column are perspectives that persons from a humanist position have expressed. We do not mean to imply that every person claiming to be a humanist would hold to every statement listed.

ACTION STEP

Evaluate which world view expresses your actions.

_____

_____

Where can you change?_____

_____

Make one positive choice to act now! What is it?

_____

_____

How will you do it?_____

_____

_____

When will you begin?_____

_____

_____

17

SPORTS AND ENTERTAINMENT:

Refreshment or Diversion?

The Atlanta Falcons were nearing the end of their first ever playoff game against the Philadelphia Eagles. The team had made a dramatic comeback with two touchdowns in the last quarter, and the clock showed only 1:39 left to play, putting the Falcons ahead 14-13. The Eagles would not quit, however, and they drove downfield and attempted a field goal with 13 seconds left. But Mike Michel's thirty-four-yard kick narrowly missed, and Atlanta fans and players began pouring onto the field in celebration.

On television, the camera zoomed in on Michel, who was stooped over, clutching his ankles as he stared at the ground in agony. Then one of the Falcons players entered the picture and extended his arms to Michel. There was no visible response from the crestfallen kicker, but that picture remained etched in viewers' minds. What could possibly divert a player from celebrating the greatest victory of his football career?

The Falcons player was Greg Brezina, a veteran of eleven NFL seasons. Having spent his entire career with Atlanta, he had enjoyed only two winning seasons. He understood how it felt to suffer defeat. One year the team had savored the promise of a championship, only to experience the bitter disappointment of two unexpected late season defeats. So Brezina could empathize with the disheartened kicker. He told Michel, "I don't know if you can understand what I'm about to say, but it doesn't really matter if you made the kick or missed it. What matters far more is if you have peace in your heart, which comes through Jesus Christ."

Several weeks later, the two players met again at a Christian conference, and Mike Michel told him, "What you did was a great example of Christ's work. I'll never forget it. And knowing Jesus Christ *is* the most important thing in my life."

Power of Entertainment

Entertainment is big business in America. In 1982 Americans spent more than 15.7 billion dollars viewing movies, attending sports events and participating in various forms of recreation.[1]

Unfortunately, much of that entertainment serves only to heighten our selfish desires rather than lift us to higher moral values. There are not enough examples of the kind of sportsmanship and personal concern that Greg Brezina displayed. Instead we read about athletes and entertainers demanding ever higher sums of money, involved in alcohol and drug use, and living lavish and often immoral life-styles far beyond the ability of most of their fans.

We do not deny the right of entertainers to enjoy the rewards that come with the employment of their skills. There is a responsibility, however, that comes with that visibility. In addition, we would like to see a return to the time when entertainment was edifying and uplifting. We are concerned about how we fill our minds, because there is a powerful principle that says what our minds think about is what we eventually become. Probably most of our readers would agree that everyone should avoid pornography. Yet we are far less cautious about other forms of entertainment, and we are subconsciously being programmed with thoughts that elevate the secular humanist world view.

Part of our concern is that we have forgotten the purpose of leisure time. Too many people work only to make enough to gain fulfillment through recreation or entertainment. But the purpose of leisure time should be to relax and rest in order for us to gain our primary fulfillment in our work.

MUSIC ONCE HAD CHARMS TO SOOTHE A SAVAGE BREAST...
NOW IT STIRS THEM UP!

James Michener, the distinguished author of *Hawaii, Space, Poland*, and many other novels, expressed similar concern in a letter to *U.S. News and World Report*. While working on a book at the University of Texas, he observed that "modern students don't read the way we used to...they are devotees of the motion pictures to a degree that startles me. My point...is that these young people are having their value systems formed by movies."[2]

Be Solution Oriented

One solution is for Christians to begin elevating the standards of our movies, sports, and other forms of entertainment. Film producer Ken Wales has produced numerous feature films such as *Revenge of the Pink Panther, Islands in the Storm, The Tamarind Seed*, and *The Prodigal*. He believes we should find ways to develop films that are outstanding in quality and make a strong effort to convey Christian values. The key to that, he explains, is "a Christian vision of life. We...need more courageous Christians in the decision-making process—as writers, directors, producers, actors. And, very important, we need Christians who are able financially to invest substantially large amounts of money in the initial development of desirable, well-done films."[3]

Through the first half of this century, movies reflected Judeo-Christian standards. Profanity was practically never heard. Romance was elevated, but sex was not explicitly flaunted. Today, too many producers justify their films by saying they give people what they want. Doing that is not good stewardship, but instead contributes to the rapid downward spiral of our culture.

Another solution is to show entertainers and athletes that they have an added responsibility as role models in society.

Athletes, actors and entertainers are highly visible, and often what they say and do can set trends for a large segment of society. That is a heavy responsibility that many do not want to bear. The lure of success, fame and fortune causes many to compromise or even reject moral values.

Greg Brezina was one who sought to do in the context of professional sports what Jesus would do. Now that Brezina is retired, he devotes his full time to communicating Christian concepts, which is the name of his organization. He demonstrates another way we can influence the entertainment industry. In December 1983, he took his three boys Christmas shopping in Fayetteville, a suburb of Atlanta, Georgia. In one store they encountered a carousel of video movies, and the boys suggested they buy one for their mother. The first film he saw was a popular soft-core porno film. Greg quickly moved his boys to another section of the store, but before they made their purchases, he realized that buying in that store would support the store's efforts to sell pornography.

"It was a good opportunity to teach the boys the difference between preference and conviction," he wrote in his monthly newsletter. "Preference says that I would rather not spend my money here, but since I will be inconvenienced by going somewhere else, I'll shop here. Conviction says principle is greater than inconvenience and worthy of sacrifice. After putting the articles back on the shelves, I asked to see the store manager. The manager said that he did not agree with selling the movie, but that he just worked here."

Greg might have let it rest there, but a few days later he called the division office of this chain of stores. The division manager said this was a pilot project and that he appreciated the feedback. He would see that the offensive movies were removed from the stores. All of us can follow Greg's example. Individually, it might not seem like much. But, if we all did our part, we could make an impact. Let's not leave it to someone else. Let's each do what we can.[4]

Think too about your local as well as national entertainers. Who is reaching them for Christ? Who is helping these people grow spiritually? Thank God for ministries[5] that aim to reach this group. But why not get involved yourself?

You may not be an entertainer, but you know them. You can pray, build relationships, share your faith, start a Bible study, and much more. Ask God to allow you to minister in this area.

Humanistic View	Biblical View
1. Get as much as you can as fast as you can	Be a good steward of your health and financial resources
2. Aim to win and become popular	Do your best, as unto the Lord
3. Do what you are told to do and don't ask questions	Provide a godly model to follow
4. Be flexible in your ethical standards (compromise) to succeed	Stand by biblical convictions regardless of the cost; that *is* true success

In this comparison chart, the points listed in the humanistic view column are perspectives that persons from a humanist position have expressed. We do not mean to imply that every person claiming to be a humanist would hold to every statement listed.

ACTION STEP

1. Write down *your standards* for entertainment in your home. What will you watch? What will you not watch?

_____

_____

2. Identify an entertainer with whom you are acquainted. Pray that someone will share the gospel with him.

_____

18

SCIENCE AND TECHNOLOGY:

Whose Arsenal, Ours or the Enemy's?

George Washington Carver was a beautiful example of someone who used his outstanding intellect for the glory of God. He was considered the world's top authority on peanuts and sweet potatoes, and developed more than 300 products from the peanut and 118 from the sweet potato. "I love the Lord Jesus, and He tells me what to do," Carver testified. When he was awarded the Roosevelt Medal in 1939, the citation read: "To a scientist humbly seeking the guidance of God and a liberator to men of the white race as well as the black."[1]

Science Has a Foundation

The realm of science is one that allows us virtually unlimited possibilities for learning about God's wonderful creation. Unfortunately, there are many who would rob us of that joy by insisting—against all sorts of evidence—that life is simply a process of evolution.

The apostle Paul wrote in Colossians 2:3 that in God "are hidden all the treasures of wisdom and knowledge." We have the exciting privilege of uncovering the truth of God's universe. Nearly every day, we gain more evidence to confirm the claims of Scripture.

John Herschel, son of Sir William Herschel, a world-famous astronomer, discovered more than five hundred new nebulae during the 1800s and also cataloged the stars and nebulae of both the Northern and Southern Hemispheres. He wrote, "All human discoveries seem to be made only for the purpose of confirming more and more strongly the truths come from on high and contained in the sacred writings."[2]

Charles Stine, an organic chemist and for many years director of research for the DuPont Company, felt that same excitement about the creator:

> The world about us, far more intricate than any watch, filled with checks and balances of a hundred varieties, marvelous beyond even the imagination of the most skilled scientific investigator, this beautiful and intricate creation, bears the signature of its Creator, graven in its works.[3]

We would like to see a return to the joy of scientific discovery from a Judeo-Christian perspective. More and more reputable scientists are rising up and acknowledging that there is a creator, even if they do not acknowledge the God of the Bible. Sir Fred Hoyle, an eminent physicist and astronomer, is one of the leading spokesmen: "The entire structure of orthodox biology still holds that life arose at random. Yet as biochemists discover more and more about the awesome complexity of life, it is apparent that the chances of it originating by accident are so minute that they can be completely ruled out. Life cannot have arisen by chance."[4]

In the search for truth, scientists must come to grips with the fact that there are two kinds of truth—observational and revealed. For many years, revealed truth, which comes only from God and answers the basic questions of life, was the basis for observational truth, which God allows us to discover for ourselves. Today most scientists assume there is only one kind of truth: that which they can observe. The result is what J. Stanley Oakes, Jr., calls "A high frontier society of geniuses producing moral pygmies who are confused and befuddled by the choices of a technological age."[5]

Professor Chandra Wickramasinghe, who has coauthored several scientific books with Fred Hoyle, isolates another problem of modern science: the fact that it is "so highly compartmentalized."

> Evolutionary biologists don't understand physics, they don't understand anything but evolutionary biology. But the universe doesn't respect the boundaries between different disciplines. The differences between biology and astronomy and chemistry and so on, these are man made artifacts of thinking. I think the whole system is doomed unless one decides that all these barriers are cleared. And I will go further to say that even the interface between theology and the other disciplines is necessary.[6]

The New Frontier in Intelligence

Recently Bill participated in a symposium at Yale University titled "Artificial Intelligence (AI) and the Human Mind." Nineteen of the world's leading scholars gathered to discuss the potential of AI.

In summary, here are their conclusions: (1) Man is an entirely material being. (2) Since man is material, he can, in principle, be duplicated and perhaps surpassed by complex robots and computer systems. (3) Thus, the concept of man having a soul or a creator is superfluous.

The danger presently lies in the prestige the AI Movement has. First, science is viewed as the most powerful intellectual force for realizing the claims of AI pioneers. Second, the work of AI is being carried on in the most prestigious universities in America. And third, most of the major science journals have accepted the premises of the secular AI researchers.

These ideas are not new, but coupled with the prestige of the AI movement and its advocates, there is a threat to Christianity if we fail to effectively combat this movement and provide biblical answers to their assumptions. When Darwin first presented his theory of evolution, it was not resisted by any major Christian thinkers of his time. As a result, it became the dominant ideology of his century. Some Christian scholars see AI becoming the dominant ideology of this century and, perhaps, having a sweeping negative impact on thought like the Darwinian theory of evolution had in the past century.

The New Frontier in Ethics

Finally, not only do we need to re-establish the connection between the creator and our exploration of His creation, but we also need to recognize the stewardship we have of new technologies. The incredible knowledge explosion, including the development of computers and sophisticated communications systems, requires much of us. We cannot begin to address the moral and ethical questions in such diverse areas as ecology, nuclear power, robotics, and genetics without a concrete value system.

NEWS ITEM : CALIFORNIA REJECTS TEXTBOOKS THAT WATER DOWN EVOLUTION.

Sir John Eccles, a Nobel laureate in medicine and physiology and a pioneer in brain research, recognizes this fact:

> We need to discredit the belief held by many scientists that science will ultimately deliver the final truth about everything. Science doesn't deliver the truth; what it provides are hypotheses in an attempt to get nearer to truth.
>
> Science also cannot explain the existence of each of us as a unique self, nor can it answer such fundamental questions as: Who am I? Why am I here? How did I come to be at a certain place and time? What happens after death? These are all mysteries that are beyond science.
>
> Science has gone too far in breaking down man's belief in his spiritual greatness and has given him the belief that he is merely an insignificant animal who has arisen by chance and necessity on an insignificant planet lost in the great cosmic immensity.[7]

We issue a call to the advancement of science and technology based not on humanistic philosophy, but on the fact that this is God's creation and He has told us to "fill the earth and subdue it; and rule over the fish of the sea and over the birds of the sky, and over every living thing that moves on the earth."[8] God holds us accountable for how we, as Christians, carry out this mandate.

Humanistic View	Biblical View
1. Technology is its own justification and is one of the keys to evolutionary salvation	Science is discovering God's creative design and utilizing that to benefit mankind
2. Science defines the laws	Science discovers the order that God has already put into the system
3. All reality and life can be explained in materialistic terms excluding any supernatural ideas (secular humanism)	Life can be defined only with God, the supernatural aspects and spiritual aspects included
4. The universe can be explained as matter plus time plus chance and is "controlled" by the process of natural evolution	The universe is explained by a personal creator God who providentially directs the affairs of the universe

In this comparison chart, the points listed in the humanistic view column are perspectives that persons from a humanist position have expressed. We do not mean to imply that every person claiming to be a humanist would hold to every statement listed.

ACTION STEP

Do you have *biblical convictions* on euthanasia, abortion, evolution, and other moral issues? What are they?

How do you defend them?

19

YOU CAN MAKE A DIFFERENCE

Have we made our point? Have we really communicated with you? Perhaps by now you have begun to feel the pain we experience concerning the fact that we are at war. We have not attempted to speak as experts in all areas, nor have we spoken of other areas about which we are concerned. But we wanted to share these concerns and challenge Christians to solidify their commitment to Christ and live out their faith in their personal and professional lives. We are increasingly hopeful that men and women are becoming aware of the ongoing warfare and are willing and determined to make a difference by joining in the battle for biblical values.

Again, we reiterate our basic contentions. First, there is a warfare going on all around us all the time for the minds and hearts of men. The enemy, Satan, is battling on every front for the lives of men and women. Often, knowingly or unknowingly, Christians even aid Satan's kingdom. We need to remember there is no safe neutral ground. If we are not actively serving God's kingdom of light, we aid the enemy's kingdom of darkness, by default or purposely, by our attitudes and actions.

Think of Satan's deceptive and subtle strategy. He begins with the mind. If Satan can pervert, confuse, divert, or even dull the minds of men and women, Christians and non-Christians alike, he has gained a victory.

For as a mind goes, so goes an individual life. As a life goes, so go a marriage and family. As a family goes, so goes the church, the body of Christ. As the church goes, so goes society.

If the church continues to lose its saltiness and brightness, there is little hope in this or any other country for a healthy, thriving society.

But we are encouraged and, in fact, confident that we can change our world. We do not use the same power techniques of the world's system, which are based on expediency and deception. Instead, we allow God to make us salt and light as He first transforms us individually, beginning with our minds. His principle is love—tough love: the kind of love that perseveres; the kind of love the apostle Paul wrote of in 1 Corinthians 13; the kind of love that starts in the mind and results in a determination and a commitment to stand tall in Christ's victory.

As our minds are brought into conformity to Christ, our values and ultimately our life-styles and conduct are changed. As these are changed, our marriages and families and relationships will change. As these are changed, our churches will be changed, and as they are changed, our society will be changed.

As we allow the Spirit of the resurrected Lord Jesus Christ to transform us as individuals through refocusing our minds, we will cease becoming "*of* the world." Then, as we are progressively transformed by the risen Christ living within us, we can launch out as salt and light and become more active "*in* the world."

We can stand up, speak lovingly and boldly, and use every biblically acceptable vehicle possible to help change our world. And we can believe that our world will be changed.

We cannot and must not sit back and let the anti-biblical world system determine the prevailing values of our day. We must change, and we can. We have tried to illustrate how people in various spheres of influence are effecting change now.

We will never have a perfect world, with imperfect man, until the Lord returns. And we do not believe the righteous are going to usher in the the kingdom of God, as some in the body of Christ believe. But that does not mean we should sit back idly and let our society deteriorate. On the contrary, we believe we are a part of a growing consensus of Bible-believing Christians who do want to see our world changed. We want to be salt and light because of our devotion to our Lord and Savior, Jesus Christ, and our love and compassion for people. Our Lord admonished us to "work as long as it is day; night is coming when no man can work" (John 9:4). We must work until Christ returns.

We must be wise and prudent in our penetration strategies. We must not neglect the God-ordained external restraints of evil, such as corporal discipline, restitution, and capital punishment. External restraints of law and government will always be necessary because we live in a world where all men are sinful by nature. But our priorities and our strategies must concentrate on changing men from the inside through the gospel. That is transformation! Without a new birth—a spiritual one—there can be no transformation. That is why evangelism is so necessary to our strategic impact.

But we also need to break out of our "Christian ghetto" mentality. We must be involved in changing society but by more than just organizing ourselves to pressure others to conform to our way of thinking and behaving. We must not settle for only external victories, which will be short-lived, unless we also help change the hearts and minds of people. We must share Paul's concern, as stated in Colossians 1:28, that we help and train people to grow and mature in Christ.

If ever you plan to do anything for Christ and His kingdom, you must do it now—"Only one life, 'twill soon be past; only what's done for Christ will last." Remember, life is but a vapor. Be sure you spend your vapor wisely. A poem we learned long ago says it well:

I counted dollars, while God counted crosses.
I counted gains while He counted losses.
I counted my worth by things gained in store,
He sized me up by the scars that I bore.
I coveted honors and sought degrees,
He wept as He counted the hours on my knees.
I never knew until one day by the grave,
How vain are the things that we spend life to
   save.

                    Author Unknown

Appendix A

I n the life of every Christian there arise various problems that need an answer, decision, or plan of action. Often the old answers just do not fit or seem appropriate anymore; or maybe we do not even know what the old answers are.

As a Christian who confesses Jesus Christ as Lord and who believes the Bible, you will want to base your answers on the solid foundation of a biblical world and life view.

What is a world view? All people regardless of geographic location and background have one. It is the basic assumptions and presuppositions one uses to organize his thoughts and feelings. A world view is the grid through which one interprets reality. All people seek to find meaning in their existence and seek to impose order on the external world, which otherwise might seem chaotic and senseless. These basic principles, which are most often taken for granted, are the building blocks of one's world view, and they govern one's system of values.

There are three major philosophical world views which are prominent in the Western world today: secular humanism, cosmic humanism, and biblical Christianity.

Secular humanism denies the existence of God; instead, it makes man the measure of all things. It places reason above revelation and subscribes to evolution over creation. Secular humanism places all its hope in "evolving" man and society.

Cosmic humanism denies the existence of the material world and a god that is separate from the created universe. Like the secular humanistic world view, man becomes the measure of all things and evolution is subscribed to over creation. Experience is placed above both reason and revelation. Cosmic humanism places its hope in the "evolving spiritual order."

Biblical Christianity affirms the personal God who created and sustains the universe and sovereignly and providentially rules over men and nations. God is the measure of all things and reveals Himself to man through nature, man's conscience, Scripture and Jesus Christ. Biblical Christianity places its hope in God through the Lord Jesus Christ.

Throughout the world today, there are at least seven major movements grounded in a world view:
1. biblical Christianity;
2. apostate Christianity (which includes liberalism, the cults, liberation theology, etc.);
3. socialist statism (in various forms such as: democratic socialism, Marxism, communism, and Nazism);
4. Rational Scientific Materialism, 5. New Age/Eastern mysticism;
6. Islam;
7. overt Satanism.

Our desire is to communicate a biblical world and life view which is comprehensive, consistent, prescriptive, and practical.

By *biblical*, we mean that which sees the Scriptures (the 66 books of the O.T. and N.T.) as the inerrant, final, applicable and sufficient authority by which we judge all matters. The foundation of this authority is the character, nature, attributes and actions of God.

By *world*, we mean everything outside the individual; this world, the unseen world and the world to come. It encompasses all of God's creation (the material and spiritual universe), and an understanding of man and his societal relationships, social structures, institutions, customs, values and culture.

By *life*, we mean the individual in general and particular, his inner life and total being—the whole person: body, mind, soul, heart and spirit—and his personal relationships with God, others and self.

By *view*, we mean our philosophy and understanding of truth, (which consists of two basic elements: reality and values), the nature and standards of God for His creation, His design of what is and what ought to be, and its impact on all creation, especially the individual, society and culture.

Below are some steps you can use to help you develop a response that is consistent with your confession as a Christian who believes the Bible and wants to have an impact for the Lord Jesus Christ. You need to:

A. Learn to identify and question world views by comparing them to God's view on the matter.

B. Define the area, issue or problem, with the guidance of the Holy Spirit, and develop a list of specific statements and general principles from the Bible on this area, issue or problem.

C. Assess the conclusions of others and compare them with your conclusions.

D. Apply the biblical perspective and your conclusion to this area, issue or problem in your life.

To have a consistent biblical world and life view, you first need to know what God has said in His Word . Study such passages as 1 John 4, 1 Timothy, 1 Thessalonians, and 2 Corinthians 11. Second, know what the world is saying. Be aware of what is going on in the world that is anti-Christian, anti-Bible and anti-God. Third, ask yourself, "What is the biblical response to these challenges?" Last, implement changes in your life in both attitudes and actions.

(For a more in-depth outline, order "How to Develop a Biblical World and Life View" and *Comparing World Views* from the Public Policy Resource Center.)

Appendix B

Paul, in 2 Corinthians 10:3-6, masterfully paints a metaphorical picture comparing speculations and reasonings with a Roman military campaign. The Roman legions were an ever-present sight throughout the Empire, so his reader could easily comprehend his analogy.

In verse 3, he acknowledges we are fleshly, that is, physical creatures; however, he says that our warfare is not physical but spiritual. It is waged in the realm of thoughts and ideas.

In verse 4, he continues the military analogy, saying our weapons of warfare are not physical, but are "divinely powerful for the destruction of fortresses." In Paul's day, most cities were walled and fortified to provide the occupants safety from outside attack. The walls were built strong and tall, and often had high towers to give defenders the advantage of elevation against would-be attackers.

What are those fortresses in the spiritual realm? In verses 5 and 6 Paul says, "We are destroying speculations and every lofty thing raised up against the knowledge of God." Here the imagery of a military onslaught by a Roman legion attacking a strongly fortified city is compared to a person's thoughts and thinking; these comprise his fortress against the truth of God. Men would rather believe lies of vain speculations than the truth about God, because to acknowledge the truth about God would place them under obligation to submit and obey God, or would cause them to feel guilty for living a life contrary to God's design. Therefore, they erect lofty towers of intellectual reasoning and haughty thoughts against arguments about the truth of God.

But Paul says our weapons of warfare are "divinely powerful for the destruction of [mental] fortresses." He more specifically deals with the believer's weaponry in Ephesians 6:10-18, which we will look at in detail later.

Back to our military imagery in 2 Corinthians 10:3-6. An attacking army first storms a fortress and its high towers—the arguments against God, which in our day include evolution, secular humanism, cosmic humanism, occultism, atheism and agnosticism. Once entrance is gained, captives are taken. This is what Paul deals with next in the second half of verse five. He says, "We are taking every thought captive to the odedience of Christ." What does that mean?

Once an army has successfully destroyed the fortifications of a city, the next move is to take its inhabitants captive. To apply this to the metaphor, it is the thoughts of a man that are raised in defense of a life-style that is in contradiction to the truth of God. Those thoughts need to be "taken captive" by being brought into obedience to Christ. That means a change in world views, a change to a biblical world view.

If a man's thoughts are not in obedience to Christ, as He said in the Sermon on the Mount, that man is guilty of breaking God's laws. God's laws are broken mentally long before they are broken in action. This is why pornography, homosexuality, and other immoralities must be combatted in the mind if there is to be any lasting victory in the actions and habits of men and women.

It is from a man's world view that his thoughts and actions come. Legislation might discourage a man from violating a specific law by his actions, but Jesus said that men are mentally guilty first of adultery and murder.

Finally, in verse 6, Paul says that once a fortress is destroyed and its occupants are taken captive, there must be a garrison left behind to guarantee no further rebellion or uprising. This is what the Romans did; they detached a garrison to patrol and guarantee peace once an area had been secured. As Paul says, "We are ready to punish all disobedience, whenever your obedience is complete."

It is one thing to win an argument, but it is quite another to change a man's world view, to get him to submit his thoughts and ideas to Christ and not raise up lofty speculations about God or His plan for man and the world.

Now let us turn our attention to the weapons of spiritual warfare that are divinely powerful in pulling down intellectual fortresses.

Looking at Ephesians 6:10-18, we find a list of armor that Paul says we are to put on in order to engage in spiritual warfare.

In verse 11 he says, "Put on the full armor of God." Here "GI" means "God's Issue," not "Government Issue." Paul uses the imagery of the Roman legionnaire, for that was the soldier of his day. The Roman legionnaire was a heavily armed soldier of the front lines. God issues the equipment, but we are to put it on; that is our responsibility. What is it we are to put on?

First, look at the nature of the warfare in which we find ourselves engaged. Paul explains that the reason we are to be fully armored is because we must be prepared to "stand" against the schemes of the devil. We are to stand as victors, for the battle is already won. The enemy has been defeated. We are on the victor's side. We, as believers, are the winners. Yet the church today acts as though we are in retreat and backed into a corner waiting for the Commander-in-Chief to rescue us by way of the rapture. Instead, ours is a hold-on mentality, not a victor's mentality.

In verse 12 of Ephesians 6, we find Paul describing the opposition. It is not flesh and blood, but it is the spiritual forces of the unseen realm. That is why we must put on "God's Issue," God's armor, all of it. Note this is a war, not a wrestling match where one opponent attempts to pin the other to the floor. It is not a game. It is war!

Next look at the armor. The first piece of armor is the belt of truth. It was the belt or girdle that held all the other pieces of equipment that were a part of the Roman soldier's armament. What is truth? It is God's Word! No wonder the enemy has leveled his heaviest attack at the Bible, particularly at biblical inerrancy. He has been doing it from the beginning. Remember in the Garden he asked Eve, "Indeed, has God said?" Without a strong conviction that the Bible *is* the Word of God and is without error, the believer is vulnerable and without a secure belt to hold the remainder of his armament together.

Second is the breastplate of righteousness, which covers the vital organs. True righteousness comes only from Christ, and it is ours by faith, by trusting in His atoning work. It is the center of all saving truth. Where do we get this knowledge? From God's Word. Where else?

Third, the soldier is to have his feet shod with the gospel of peace. Peace with God is the result of our trust in Christ. When you know you are right and you stand for the truth, there is no doubting in your heart and mind; you can stand firm against the onslaughts of the enemy, such as intellectual arguments. If you are not sure of your salvation or not sure God's Word is absolutely true, then you are unstable and subject to be swayed by the deception of the enemy.

Fourth is the shield of faith. R.C.H. Lenski points out the Greek definite article, which the English translators have left out. Instead of "the shield of faith" it should read "the shield of *the* faith." The distinction is between the objective nature of "the faith" versus the subjectivity of "faith." "The faith" is a body of propositional truths embodied in Christian doctrines, and is more fitting for the weaponry of the believer. For he stands on the truth of Scripture.

It is our failure to stand on the truth of Scripture

that makes us susceptible to the "flaming missiles of the evil one." The flaming missles are doubts—doubts about truth, doubts about one's salvation, doubts about God's Word, doubts about God. They are extinguished by the affirmation—"I believe!" Jesus combated the devil's attacks by quoting Scripture—truth always dispels doubt and darkness. Truth gives light. Believing is not enough, for faith *must* have an object and the object *is* God's Word, written and incarnate.

Fifth is the helmet of salvation. Again Lenski says the definite article is absent in the English translation. "The salvation" is our present salvation which saves and keeps us safe, and protects the head from a fatal and disabling blow. It is the mind that is the battleground for spiritual warfare.

Those five pieces of spiritual armor are defensive. The sixth issue is the sword of the Spirit. The Greek word is "rhema" or "the utterance of God." Jesus quoted Scripture to the devil, and this forced him to flee; therefore, Scripture memorization *is essential* to spiritual warfare, for it is an offensive weapon God has placed at the believer's disposal to use against the enemy.

All the elements of armor are God's Word. The last issue is not a part of our armor, but is our communication system. It puts the believer in contact with his Commander-in-Chief, and it is always available in time of need. It is prayer and petition. We are to be in constant contact with our Commander-in-Chief if we expect to "stand" on the victory He has already secured. Ours is to occupy the defeated fortresses and strongholds that He has pulled down.

So a biblical world view is absolutely essential for waging spiritual warfare. Obviously, God's Word *is* our arsenal against all other world views.

The following sources were helpful in gathering these insights into 2 Corinthians 10:3-6 and Ephesians 6:10-18:

W. E. Vine *An Expository Dictionary of New Testament Words.* Westwood, NJ: Fleming H. Revell, 1940.

Marvin R. Vincent. *Word Studies in the New Testament, Vol. III: The Epistles of Paul.* Grand Rapids, MI:

Eerdmans, 1946.

Henry Alford. *The Greek New Testament, Vol. II: Acts, Romans, Corinthians*. Revised by Everett F. Harrison. Chicago: Moody, 1968.

R.C.H. Lenski. *The Interpretion of First and Second Corinthians, and Interpretation of Galatians, Ephesians, & Philippians*. Minneapolis: Augsburg, 1937 and 1963.

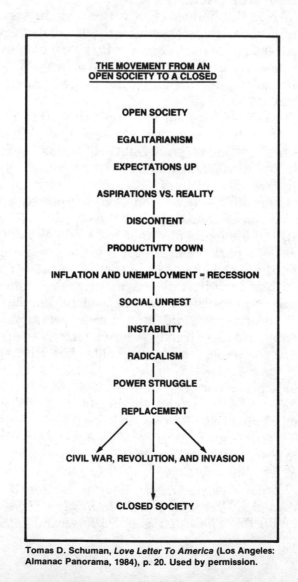

THE MOVEMENT FROM AN OPEN SOCIETY TO A CLOSED

OPEN SOCIETY

EGALITARIANISM

EXPECTATIONS UP

ASPIRATIONS VS. REALITY

DISCONTENT

PRODUCTIVITY DOWN

INFLATION AND UNEMPLOYMENT = RECESSION

SOCIAL UNREST

INSTABILITY

RADICALISM

POWER STRUGGLE

REPLACEMENT

CIVIL WAR, REVOLUTION, AND INVASION

CLOSED SOCIETY

Tomas D. Schuman, *Love Letter To America* (Los Angeles: Almanac Panorama, 1984), p. 20. Used by permission.

Appendix C

How does a Christian use the element of surprise in engaging in spiritual combat? In order to answer that question we need to develop a background to understand the surprise tactic in spiritual warfare.

In Matthew 10:16, Jesus is sending the twelve out on their first trial mission on His behalf. He told them they were going out as sheep among wolves. Unthinkable! What shepherd would sacrifice his sheep in such a manner? The key to this verse is found in the pronoun, "I." It was Jesus who sent them out; therefore, He assumes responsibility for protecting them from the wolves. The wolves here represent the world. This does not mean the sheep will not be attacked; He certainly was, time and time again, especially by the religious leaders. His disciples were going to live among those of the world who held a world view different from than theirs, and this meant they would face those who held a different set of values.

So how were they to conduct themselves among wolves? Jesus quotes a proverb to them: "Be shrewd as serpents, and innocent as doves." What does this mean?

The Greek word translated "shrewd" carries the idea of prudence; understanding; having the right use of the mind; sensible. We might say using common sense. It means the ability to discern modes of action with a view to their results. Too often we, as Christians, are naive, gullible, credulous; that is, we lack discernment. Jesus says we need to be wise or prudent among wolves. We need to be students of men. We need to know what causes them to viciously attack Christians. There is no guarantee we will not be attacked when we go among wolves as sheep, but we certainly do not have to provoke the attack due to our lack of understanding.

The counterbalance to shrewdness in the proverb Jesus quoted to His disciples is a Greek word translated "innocent." The literal meaning is "unmixed; unadulterated." It is used in speaking of wine without water—in other words, wine that has not been watered down or diluted. It is used also of a metal without alloy, one that is pure.

Often we are overbalanced in either of these two qualities. Shrewdness without innocence can lead to dishonesty and falling into the world's dog-eat-dog philosophy. This is what Jesus meant by going out among wolves; that is, into the world where it is every man for himself.

Innocence without prudence or shrewdness can lead to gullibility, which is quite often the position the Christian finds himself in. To be gullible can lead to being eaten up by the wolves without realizing what is happening until it is all over.

Back to our original question: How does a Christian use the element of surprise in engaging in spiritual combat? In light of the Matthew 10:16 study, the Christian is to be a paradox. By that we mean he is to be both prudent and innocent in his dealing with "wolves" the world system.

As one reads Paul's epistles, especially those addressed to churches, he always closes by giving them specific instructions on how they should conduct themselves in the world. Perhaps the one passage that best summarizes Paul's admonition to believers on how to conduct themselves is found in the first two verses of Romans 12, a familiar passage, but one that provides the answer to our question of surprise.

The charge is not to be conformed but transformed. How? By the renewing of your mind. The Greek word translated "conformed" means to fashion or shape one thing like another. When we share the world view of the world, we will think, act, and behave like the world, and therefore, our light will be hid and our saltiness will be gone.

The second key word in this passage is the Greek word translated "transformed," which means to change into another form. We, as Christians, are undergoing a complete change which, under the power of God, will find expression in our character and conduct.

The contrast between "conformed" and "transformed" is that the former lays stress on the outward while the latter stresses the inward change. How is that inward change to be brought about? By a renewing of the mind. The Greek word translated "mind" denotes the seat of reflective consciousness, comprising the faculties of perception and understanding, as well as those of feeling, judging and determining.

What this all means is that we need to have a biblical world view; that is, the mind of Christ. In having our minds so transformed, we will be able to use the element of surprise in our spiritual combat. For example: When we think, talk, act, behave like the world because we hold the same world view, our impact is relatively low. Our light is dimmed and our saltiness is absent. But when our world view is the mind of Christ, our impact is high, for we are thinking, talking, acting and behaving, not as the world does, but as Christ would. Then the world—the wolves—are caught off guard, surprised. Once we have their attention, we can give a reason for the hope that lies within us; that is, we can explain why we are different. It is because we are being transformed rather than conformed.

The following sources were helpful in gathering these insights into how Christians can use the element of surprise in engaging in spiritual combat:

W. E. Vine. *An Expository Dictionary of New Testa-*

ment Words. Westwood, NJ: Fleming H. Revell, 1940.

Marvin R. Vicent. *Word Studies in the New Testament, Vol. I: The Synoptic Gospels, Acts of the Apostles, Epistles of Peter, James, and Jude.* Grand Rapids, Mi: Eerdmans, 1946.

Archibald Thomas Robertson. *Word Pictures in the New Testament, Vol. I: The Gospel According to Matthew, The Gospel According to Mark.* Nashville: Broadman, 1930.

R. C. H. Lenski. *The Interpretation of St. Matthew's Gospel.* Minneapolis: Augsburg, 1961.

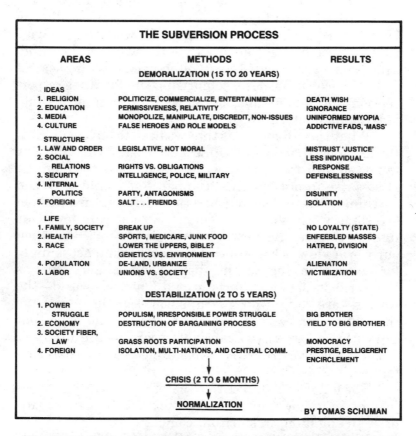

This chart shows the four stages of Soviet ideological subversion: demoralization, destabilization, crisis, and normalization. The methods used by the subverter in the different areas of life produce their desired results in a country that does not resist the subversion process.

Tomas D. Schuman, *Love Letter To America* (Los Angeles: Almanac Panorama, 1984), p. 22. Used by permission.

Appendix D

One area of contemporary society that certainly needs biblical thinking and application is the area of human life. Your response to issues such as abortion, infanticide, genocide, suicide and brutality are intrinsically related to how you view human life. Using the process described in chapter 7, we would proceed as follows:

1. Understand and analyze contemporary issues.

There are four prevalent views regarding the value of human life. The first three are a variation on the theme of materialism, that all of life and reality can be explained by only natural, materialistic means and processes. The views are:

The evolutionary view: Man is the product of evolution that began billions of years ago. As evolutionist and humanist Carl Sagan said:

> All life on earth is the same life. There are superficial differences which, understandably, seem important to us. But down deep at the heart of life, we are, all of us—redwoods and nematodes, viruses and eagles, slime molds and humans—almost identical. We are all the expressions of the interaction of proteins and nucleic acids.[1]

The behaviorist view: Man is the product of genetic

and environmental conditioning. The late Francis Schaeffer analyzed and quoted B.F. Skinner:

> Essentially, behaviorism declares that all of a person's behavior is the result of environmental conditioning, whether that conditioning occurred prior to birth and resides in the genes or subsequent to birth and resides in the external environment. As Skinner says, "Personal exemption from a complete determinism is revoked as scientific analysis progresses, particularly in accounting for the behavior of the individual." (*Beyond Freedom and Dignity*, p. 21). That is, all of an individual's actions are either predetermined by his heredity or immediately determined by his surroundings.[2]

The electro-chemical machine view: Man is a complex collection of hormones and plasmas animated by neurological activity. As Francis Schaeffer said about Frances Crick, one of the discoverers of the DNA molecule,

> A crucial part of the view of life that Francis Crick expounded...is the idea that man can be essentially reduced to the chemical and physical properties that go to make up the DNA template. That's what man is.
>
> Philosophically, therefore, Francis Crick is a reductionist—that is, one who would reduce man from a compound personal being made in the image of God to an electro-chemical machine. Unfortunately, such a notion not only makes man meaningless but soon leads to the idea that man can, and just as well may, be manipulated with impunity.[3]

The created in the image of God view: Man has value and dignity because the Creator endowed man with His own image, thus giving man a higher identity than the animals, plants, inanimate objects and the machine.

2. Given these contemporary views, observe how the Scripture views man.

- Man was created in the image of God, (Genesis 1:26,27). This gives man his inherent value and dignity.
- The fall of man marred the image of God, but man retains that image to this day (Genesis 5:1-3; 9:5,6; 1 Corinthians 11:7; James 3:9).
- The image of God can be renewed in man in time by the divine activities of regeneration and sanctification (Romans 8:29).
- Life begins at conception. David acknowledges the be-

ginning of his spiritual nature at conception (Psalm 51) and praises God for the divine workmanship and design in his pre-natal development in the womb (Psalm 139).
3. Apply the biblical perspective.

Because man has value and dignity based on the image of God imprinted in him, the following areas are prime concerns for those with a biblical perspective.

Abortion: Human life starts at conception and deserves all the protection we can give it.

Infanticide: The termination of a life in an active or passive manner, because that life does not meet some human standard of quality, directly contradicts God's valuation of men as made in His own image.

Genocide: The hatred of or attempted elimination of a race of people because of supposed "inferiority" contradicts the equal status given to all men by God, because we are all His creations, made in His own image.

Brutality: When human life is devalued by a non-biblical view of man, insensitivity and brutalization begin to characterize our attitudes and conduct toward other human beings.

---

1. Carl Sagan, "How Life Began," *Parade Magazine* (December 2, 1984).
2. Francis Schaeffer, *The Complete Works of Francis A. Schaeffer*, Vol. I: *A Christian View of Philosophy & Culture* (Westchester, IL: Crossway Books, 1982), p. 374.
3. Ibid., p. 362.

Appendix E

If the objective of 66 percent of the creators of television entertainment is to reform society according to their views, then how can we combat the intrusion into our home?

For some, the solution is to remove television sets from the home. But many people do not find that a viable alternative, for there are a few important times when there is significant programming worth watching. Others find it valuable to store the television and bring it out only for specific reasons. That approach greatly reduces the temptation to turn the set on without a specific reason.

Whatever we do, we need a plan to help us evaluate what we watch and when we watch it. The following are some questions to consider:

Before a Program

1. Why should I consider watching this program? What is the purpose of the show? How will it help me reach my spiritual goals?

2. How much time have I spent watching television this week? (The average person spends more than 35 hours per week in front of the set.)

3. Have I properly ordered my priorities? One

minimum standard might be that I spend at least as much time in the Bible as I spend watching television. Another consideration is the time I spend with members of my family. Television can rob us of valuable family time. Ask if watching this program together will help or hurt the family.

During a Program

1. What moral values are being promoted or undermined? Can I determine the world view of the main character? Of the script writer?

2. Does this program alter my thoughts about God? How? Does it give me greater compassion for people, or does it numb me to their problems and anguish?

3. What role models are being portrayed for my children? (You might make some notes to discuss with your children after the show is completed).

After a Program

1. Am I a better person for having watched this show? Should I consider watching this show again? Why? Why not?

2. How can I use this as a teaching tool for my children? How can I use this experience to draw me closer to God and to motivate me to help others?

3. Do I need to communicate my convictions about this program and its message to the producer and advertisers?

In Summary

The Christian should ask two questions before making decisions about involvement in any activity, whether watching television, attending movies, or participating in any amusement:

1. Is this *lawful* according to God's Word? (John 14:21; 15:10; Romans 3:31; 6:16; Ephesians 5:1-7). If not, the answer is simple: Don't do it! If yes, then a second question must be asked:

2. Is this *profitable*, providing the *best* benefit for

God, others and myself, according to God's standards? (Romans 14:19; 15:1-3; 1 Corinthians 6:12,13; 10:23,24). If not, then one should seriously consider not doing it ("constrained by the love of Christ," 1 Corinthians 8:9-13; 2 Corinthians 5:14). If yes, go ahead, if you can do so in faith, without doubting, and in moderation, when applicable (John 13:17; Romans 14:23; Galatians 5:23; James 4:17).

Footnotes

Chapter 1

1. Joe Bayly, *Winterflight* Waco:(Word, 1981.).

2. "Globalism," *Education Newsline* (June/July, 1985), pp. 6-7.

3. Statistics from Arthur S. DeMoss Foundation, telephone interview, February 19, 1986.

4. "Penthouse, Playboy Blame Losses on NFD", *NFD Journal* (November/December, 1985), p. 1.

5. "Thousands of Stores Get Out of Porn Business, Not 7-Eleven," *NFD Journal* (May/June, 1985), p. 1.

6. "Kroger Pulls Porn, 7-Eleven Still Says 'No!'," *NFD Journal* (January, 1985), p. 1.

7. "Albertsons Pulls Porn, 7-Eleven Says 'No!'," *NFD Journal* (February, 1985), p. 1.

8. "Thousands of Stores Get Out of Porn Business, Not

7-Eleven," *NFD Journal* (May/June, 1985), p. 1.

9. "Nurse's Prayer Suit Settled," *The Rutherford Institute* (November/December, 1985), Vol. 2, No. 5, pp. 1-2.

10. "Institute Wins Acquittal of Pro-Life Reporters," *The Rutherford Institute* (September/October, 1985), Vol. 2, No. 4, pp. 1, 6-7.

11. "Victory for Vickie Frost," *Concerned Women for America News* (August, 1985), Vol. 7, No. 8, pp. 1, 5.

12. "CWA Attorney Will Argue Case," *Concerned Women for America News* (May, 1985), Vol. 7, No. 5, pp. 1, 12.

13. "Power, Glory—And Politics," *Time* (February 17, 1986), p. 63.

14. Ibid.

15. "Turn Your Heart Toward Home," *Focus On The Family* (January, 1986), p. 2.

16. "News and Such . . .," *Focus On The Family* (June, 1985), p. 10.

Chapter 2

1. Interview, Harvey Pflug, Ft. Collins, Colorado (August, 1983).

2. On May 16, 1985, the Nally's suit against Grace Community Church was dismissed by Superior Court Judge Joseph Kalin. Judge Kalin ruled, "There is no compelling state interest for this court to interfere in the pastoral counseling activities of Grace Community Church. Such interference could result in excessive entanglement of the state in the church and re-

ligious beliefs and teachings." He went on to say, "Any attempt to 'impart standards of pastoral counseling would open the floodgates to clergy malpractice suits' and have a 'chilling effect on the exercise of freedom of religion.'" The Nallys' lawyer, Edward Baker, said he was shocked by the ruling and was ready to appeal if the parents wished to do so. San Bernardino, CA, *Sun* (May 17, 1985), Sec. A, p. 3; "News: The Nation's First 'Clergy Malpractice' Suit Goes to Trial Later This Month," *Christianity Today* (April 19, 1985), Vol. 27, No. 7, pp. 60-61.

3. "News: North American Scene," *Christianity Today* (April 20, 1984), Vol. 28, No. 7, p. 41.

4. "Children From the Laboratory," *AMA Prism* (May 1973), cited by Dr. and Mrs. J. C. Wilke in *The Handbook on Abortion* (Cincinnati: Hays, 1982), p. 113.

5. *The Charter of the President and Fellows of Harvard College,* pp. 6-7.

6. *Charter of a College to Be Erected in New Jersey, by the Name of Queen's College,* cover.

7. David Manuel and Peter Marshall, *The Light and the Glory* (Old Tappan, NJ: Fleming H. Revell, 1977), pp. 289, 323, 326, 339.

8. Ibid., pp 342-43.

9. Thomas Jefferson, *The Writings of Thomas Jefferson* (1892, 1899), Compiled by Paul Leicester Ford, Vol. 1, p. 447; cited by *Freeman Digest: Thomas Jefferson* (1981), p. 92: cited by John Eidsmoe, *The Christian Legal Advisor* (Milford, MI: Mott Media, 1984), p. 142.

10. B. F. Morris, *Christian Life and Character of the Civil Institutions of the United States* (Philadelphia: G. C. Childs, 1864), p. 35: cited by Anson Phelps Stokes

and Leo Pfeffer, *Church and State in the United States* (Evanston: Harper & Row, 1950, 1964), p. 55: cited by John Eidsmoe, *The Christian Legal Advisor* (Milford, MI: Mott Media, 1984), p. 392.

11. Proclamation by President Abraham Lincoln, (April 30, 1863), p. 5, paragraphs 4-5, p. 6, paragraphs 1-2.

12. James C. Hefley, *America: One Nation Under God* (Wheaton, IL: Victor Books, 1969), pp. 10-11.

13. Ibid.

14. Ray Stannard Baker and William E. Dede, eds., *Public Papers of Woodrow Wilson* (New York: Harper, 1925), Vol. II, p. 302.

15. Charles Hurd, ed., *A Treasury of Great American Quotations* (New York: Hawthorn, 1964), p. 257.

16. Deuteronomy 28:1,7-10,15 (Living Bible).

17. God desires that His own attribute of righteousness be expressed in people and nations. God's character transcends any time or political boundary and so is applicable to all times, peoples, nations. God has used law to prove to men that they lack God's righteousness and can never achieve His standard in their own strength and wisdom. Law has never provided mercy, satisfaction, justification or enablement to meet God's righteous standard. However, through grace, God's righteousness has been satisfied in Christ, and His righteousness can be accounted to the individual through faith in Christ and now Christians can fulfill the righteousness of the Law ("that the requirement of the Law might be fulfilled in us," Romans 8:4). That righteousness can now be fulfilled by the Christian in the power of the Holy Spirit ("who do not walk according to the flesh, but according to the Spirit," Romans 8:4).

On the basis of His own righteousness and standards, God makes His judgments on society. If society obeys and conforms to His righteous standards, He will bring blessing; if it disobeys and rebels, He brings cursing and judgment. This is applicable to all cultures, civilizations, nations and ethnic groups. None can escape from God's standards based on His own character. Examples of God's standards being applied to both the chosen nation, Israel, as well as Gentile nations include: "Righteousness exalts a nation, but sin is a disgrace to any people," (Proverbs 14:34); God's judgment on Sodom and Gomorrah for their moral sin (Genesis 19); Jonah's going to preach repentance to the Ninevites because of their violations of God's law; David's concern to communicate God's "testimonies" to other kings (Psalm 119:46); Amos pronouncing judgment on Gentile nations in 1:3—2:3, because they have violated God's Law, just as Judah and Israel have. The implication is that God's righteous standards have jurisdiction over all nations, not just Israel.

18. "Working mothers with children under 18:
    1950 - 18.4 percent
    1960 - 27.6 percent
    1970 - 39.7 percent
    1980 - 54.1 percent
    The number of employed mothers whose children are under six was 48.7 percent in 1982, compared with 11.9 percent in 1950. And of the mothers of school-age children, nearly two-thirds have jobs outside the home today."

    Mary Stewart Van Leeuwen, "The End of Female Passivity," Christianity Today Institute, "Into the Next Century: Trends Facing the Church" (January 17, 1986), p. 12-I.

19. Possibly including Canada and South Korea.

20. We find an alarming overreaction today on the part of many Christians to those who want to see America reflect God's righteous standards, fearful that some of these people may desire to set up a theocracy (ruled by God as a chosen nation such as Israel was). Whereas, we do *not* believe America is a modern age Israel, we do believe this country is worth praying and fighting for. We think God deplores any *cynicism* and *sarcasm* toward this country, often typified by those who react to such groups as the Moral Majority.

21. *Webster's New Twentieth Century Dictionary, Unabridged* (New York, Simon and Schuster, 1983), p. 1553.

22. A.P. Fitt, *The Life of D.L. Moody* (Chicago: Moody, n.d.), p. 48; cited in *Worldwide Challenge* (May/June, 1984), p. 9.

23. Francis Schaeffer, *A Christian Manifesto* (Westchester, IL: Crossway, 1981), p. 17.

Chapter 3

1. Garth Lean, *Brave Men Choose* (London: Blandford Press, 1961), p. 14.

2. Ibid., pp. 36-38.

3. "By draining the market of capital that would otherwise be used for investment, the government causes a decrease in the number of new jobs, a fall in productivity, and a long-term decline in the nation's standard of living.

   "Money to new businesses is choked off, and the economy can't grow."

Michael Fries and C. Holland Taylor, *A Christian Guide to Prosperity* (Oakland: Communications Research, 1984), p. 220.

4. Ibid.

5. Theodore H. White, *In Search of History: A Personal Approach* (New York: Warner Books, 1978), p. 4.

6. John C. Wu, *Fountain of Justice* (China: Mei Ya, 1980).

   Available from:
   International Scholarly Book Service, Inc.
   P.O. Box 1632
   Beaverton, OR 97075

7. Kenneth Scott Latourette, *A History of The Expansion of Christianity*, Vol. III (Grand Rapids: Zondervan, 1970), p. 399.

8. David Breese, *Seven Men Who Rule the World From the Grave* (Oklahoma City: Southwest Radio Church, 1980), pp. 8-9.

9. William J. Murray, *My Life Without God* (Nashville: Thomas Nelson, 1982), p. 75.

10. Ibid., p. 86.

11. Concerned Women for America has a larger membership than the National Organization for Women (NOW), the Women's Political Caucus, and the League of Women Voters combined.

Chapter 4

1. Romans 12:2 (J.B. Phillips translation).

2. Herbert Lockyer, *Last Words of Saints and Sinners* (Grand Rapids, MI: Kregel, 1975), p. 132.

3. Paul Kurtz, *In Defense of Secular Humanism* (Buffalo: Prometheus, 1983), pp. 8-9.

4. Paul Kurtz, ed., *Humanist Manifestos I and II* (Buffalo: Prometheus, 1973), p. 10.

5. Roy Torcaso wanted to become a notary public in Montgomery County, Maryland, but refused to affirm a belief in God. So, his request was denied. He sued on the grounds his First Amendment rights were being violated. The United States Supreme Court sided with Torcaso, saying no government can constitutionally force any person to profess a belief or disbelief in any religion. The Court, in a footnote, went on to say that some religions do not believe in God, and specifically named Secular Humanism as one of them.

6. *Human Manifestos I and II*, pp. 16,17,18,23.

7. Swami Vivekananda, *Inspired Talks* (New York: Ramakrisna Vivekananda Center, 1958), p. 218; cited in SCP Journal, (Winter, 1981-82), footnote p. 6.

8. Health care focused on the whole person, physical and spiritual, with emphasis on preventive care, is Christian when it is guided by God's Word. However, under the label of holistic health (lower case 'h'), the world view of Eastern mysticism and pantheism has been introduced. See note on Paul C. Reisser, M.D., *The Holistic Healers: A Christian Perspective on New-Age Health Care,* in the bibliography for Chapter 4.

9. Douglas R. Groothuis, *Unmasking the New Age* (Downers Grove, IL: InterVarsity Press, 1986).

10. John N. Oswalt, "The Old Testament and Homosex-

uality," Chapter 1; Charles W. Keysor, ed. *What You Should Know About Homosexuality*, (Grand Rapids: Zondervan Publishing House, 1979), pp. 24-25.

11. Cited by John W. Whitehead, *The Second American Revolution* (Elgin, IL: David C. Cook, 1982), p. 31.

12. Alexis de Tocqueville, *Democracy in America*, p. 291; quoted by John Whitehead, *Second American Revolution* (Westchester, IL: Crossway, ed., 1985), p. 34.

13. Hugo Grotius, cited by Rosalie J. Slater in *Teaching and Learning America's Christian History* (San Francisco: Foundation for American Education, 1965), p. 69.

14. Ephesians 5:15,16.

15. Matthew 6:33.

16. Colossians 3:17.

17. Ephesians 6:7,8.

18. 1 Corinthians 10:31.

Chapter 5

1. William Morris, ed., *The American Heritage Dictionary of the English Language* (Boston: Houghton Mifflin, 1969).

2. Ephesians 5:8; 1 John 5:11,12; 3:10.

3. Acts 26:18; Colossians 1:13; 1 Peter 2:9,10.

4. 1 Corinthians 7:5; 2 Corinthians 11:13-15; 4:3,4; Revelation 12:10.

5. John 1:9-13; 3:1-21; Romans 8:9-11; Colossians 1:13.

6. 2 Corinthians 10:3-5; Ephesians 6:13-18; 1 Peter 5:8,9.

7. A. W. Tozer, "This World: Playground or Battleground?" from *The Best of A. W. Tozer* (Grand Rapids: Baker, 1978), pp. 84-86.

8. *The American Heritage Dictionary*.

9. Romans 12:1,2; Colossians 1:13.

10. Philippians 3:4, 7-10.

11. Psalm 46:10.

12. Acts 5:29; Ephesians 6:6.

13. Mark 8:38; Colossians 3:23,24.

14. Zechariah 4:6.

15. James 1:2-7.

16. Philippians 4:4-8.

17. Galatians 5:22,23; Ephesians 5:18; 1 Peter 2:9,10.

18. Philippians 3:20.

19. 1 John 2:3,4.

20. Isaiah 14:12-20; Ezekiel 28:11-15. "Lucifer" comes from the Hebrew word *helel* which means "brightness," or "shining one." "This designation, referred to Satan, is coupled with the epithet 'son of the morning' and clearly signifies 'bright star' (Isa. 14:12-14), probably what we call the 'morning star.'" *Unger Bible Dictionary* (Chicago: Moody, 1957), p. 670.

21. Revelation 12:4,9.

22. Donald Grey Barnhouse, *The Invisible War* (Grand Rapids: Zondervan, 1965), p. 44.

23. Romans 8:28,29.

24. Matthew 6:33.

25. Barnhouse, *The Invisible War*, p. 83.

26. Isaiah 14:15,16.

27. Galatians 2:20.

28. Matthew 6:33.

29. "My purpose is to give life in all its fullness." John 10:10 (The Living Bible).

30. "We are ambassadors for Christ," 2 Corinthians 5:20.

31. *HIS* (March, 1983), Vol. 43, No. 6, back cover.

32. Galatians 5:19-21.

33. Francis Schaeffer, *The Great Evangelical Disaster* (Westchester, IL: Crossway, 1984), pp. 50-51.

34. Cited in *Progress* (February, 1985), p. 9.

Chapter 6

1. Reporter's Investigation: Osseo, Minnesota. See also "Religion and School," *Minnesota News Tribune* (October 19, 1981).

2. "ACLU Seeks Removal of Crosses, Star." *Houston Chronicle* (January 6, 1982), Section 1.

3. Peggy Lamson, *Roger Baldwin: Founder of the American Civil Liberties Union* (Boston: Houghton Mifflin Co., 1976), pp. 190-91 (emphasis in original).

4. James I. Wilson, *The Principles of War* (Annapolis: Christian Books, 1964).

5. 1 Corinthians 9:24.

6. Matthew 28:19,20. Sharing the gospel and fulfilling the Great Commission will not only transform individual lives but will also transform society. Christ's mandate includes His universal power, authority and sovereignty, as given Him by God the Father (Luke 24:50ff; 1 Corinthians 15:24ff; Ephesians 1:20ff; Philippians 2:9ff; Hebrews 1:3), rightfully exercised in heaven and on earth, so that all the nations are discipled. This is more than one-to-one or even small group discipleship, as effective as these have been. Certainly, social change always starts in the spirit of the individual. The social arenas of life are changed through spiritual renewal in individuals. But redemption of society, its institutions, professions, trades, disciplines and associations, for the glory of God, must also be our goal. As Joseph Morecraft states,

"Consistent Bible-believing Christians work to reconstruct

culture and society in the power of the Holy Spirit, directed by the Word of God, to the glory of God, because they believe that Christ came to *rescue* culture and history, *not* to discard them," (Joseph C. Morecraft, III, "The Great Commission," in *Dominion Network,* Vol. 1, No. 1, January/February, 1985, p. 2).

7. So, in addition to evangelism and discipleship for individuals and small groups, there must be the strategic planning needed to impact nations, corporations, institutions and professions to produce fruitful, influential, ministry-oriented, biblical-world-view-equipped leaders to serve the kingdom of Christ and thus help fulfill the Great Commission.

8. Luke 14:25-33.

9. Romans 12:2.

10. Banjit Singh and Do-Wang Mei, *Theory & Practice of Modern Guerrilla Warfare* (New York: Asia, 1971), p. 28.

11. Ibid. p. 31.

12. Charles Thayer, *Guerrilla* (New York: Harper and Row, 1963), p. 39, cited by Singh and Mei, *Theory and Practice.*

13. General Karl von Clausewitz, cited by Wilson, *The Principles of War*; pg. 29.

14. Singh and Mei, *Guerrilla Warfare*, p. 44-45.

15. 2 Corinthians 2:11.

16. James 5:12.

17. Matthew 10:16.

18. John 17:21 (The Living Bible).

19. *Dictionary of U.S. Military Terms,* published by the Joint Chiefs of Staff, (June, 1948); cited by Wilson, *The Principles of War,* p. 48.

20. General Karl von Clausewitz, *Principles of War,* cited by Wilson, p. 53.

21. Judges 7:1-25.

22. *Winston S. Churchill, His Complete Speeches, 1897-1963* (London: Chelson House, 1974), p. 6499.

Chapter 7

1. Quoted by John Powell, *Abortion: The Silent Holocaust* (Allen, TX: Argus Communications, 1981), p. 30.

2. Colossians 1:16.

3. Romans 12:1,2.

4. C. S. Lewis, *Mere Christianity* (New York: MacMillan, 1960), p. 31.

5. Matthew 22:36-40.

6. Acts 17:11.

7. Too often, people want to understand fully before they decide to obey God's Word. God's desire is for men to obey what He says, then God will give man further understanding. Knowledge without obedience leads to pride (1 Corinthians 8:1), but knowledge tempered by obedience leads to maturity. Paul's prayer for the church at Philippi, recorded in Philippians 1:9,10, is one that applies to all Christians, "that your love may abound still more and more in real knowledge and all discernment, so that you may approve the things that are excellent." This prayer is answered in Christians who have greater discernment and are able to choose between good and evil and between good and excellent.

   Also, in Hebrews 5:11-14, immaturity in Christian living and thinking is challenged because, by now, some of the church "ought to be teachers." Instead of weakness, the author of the epistle to the Hebrews exhorts a strengthening exercise or practice of wisdom that builds the ability to discern "good from evil." This training is necessary for maturity and the ability to evaluate situations and issues from a biblical perspective.

8. 2 Timothy 3:16,17.

9. John 10:35.

10. James W. Sire, *How to Read Slowly* (Downers Grove, IL: InterVarsity, 1978), p. 15.

11. Colossians 3:2.

12. For more information, read Ron Jenson's short book, *Biblical Meditation: A Transforming Discipline,* (Oakland, CA: ICBI Press, 1982).

13. Interview, (February 15, 1985).

Chapter 8

1. "My little children, I am writing these things to you that you may not sin. And if anyone sins, we have an Advocate with the Father, Jesus Christ the righteous; and He Himself is the propitiation for our sins; and not for ours only, but also for those of the whole world. And by this we know that we have come to know Him, if we keep His commandments. The one who says, 'I have come to know Him,' and does not keep His commandment, is a liar, and the truth is not in him; but whoever keeps His word, in him the love of God has truly been perfected. By this we know that we are in Him" (1 John 2:1-5). Romans 7 also contains the same idea.

2. Matthew 5:13, 16; John 17:21.

3. John 17.

4. "Religion still plays a role, however. In the *U.S. News* survey, 38 percent of adults under 30, about half of those 30 to 44, and 60 percent of those over 45 said religion affected their ethical and moral behavior 'a great deal.'

"Yet pollster George Gallup, Jr. told a Christian symposium on November 2 (1985), 'Church attendance makes little difference in people's ethical views and behavior with respect to lying, cheating, pilferage and not reporting theft.'"

U.S. News & World Report (December 9, 1985), p. 57.

5. Romans 12:1,2.

6. Juan Carlos Ortiz, *Disciple* (Wheaton, IL: Creation

House, 1975).

7. 1 Peter 3:15.

8. John 1:5.

9. John 14:6.

10. John 8:12 (The Living Bible).

Chapter 9

1. Richard M. Weaver, *Ideas Have Consequences* (Chicago: University of Chicago, 1948), p. 121.

2. J. B. Phillips, *Letters to Young Churches* (New York: MacMillan, 1947), p. xiv.

3. John 15:7.

4. "Inquiry," *USA Today* (Wednesday, October 10, 1984), p. 11A.

5. Ibid.

6. John 13:34,35 (The Living Bible).

7. Matthew 6:33 19,20.

8. The Hebrew word *ebed* carries the idea of service by choice. If a Hebrew was unable to pay his debts, he offered himself to his fellow countryman as a slave. God gave Israel specific instructions regarding their treatment of slaves. The length of service by a Hebrew slave was, at most, six years, for every seventh year was a sabbatical year in which Hebrew slaves were set free.

   In Exodus 21:1-6 and Leviticus 25:39-43, a Hebrew slave, who enjoyed serving his master and was to be set free but chose to continue serving because he loved his master, became a bond-slave or bond-servant. The master would take his slave and pierce his ear so he was identified as a bond-slave, a slave by choice. In the New Testament, the Greek word *doulos* also carries the idea of one who gives himself up to the will of another. Paul used this term of himself as he called himself a bond-servant of Christ Jesus in his introduction to his letter to the Romans. He also told the church at Corinth that they were bought with a price, therefore, they were not slaves of men and their own lustful appetites, but were now slaves of Christ to serve the cause of righteousness (1 Corinthians 6:19; 7:22,23).

In Romans 6:16, Paul says we are all slaves, either of sin or of righteousness.

9. Matthew 16:24.

10. Matthew 6:24.

11. Interview with Bob Davenport (January 29, 1985).

Chapter 10

1. George Barna and William Paul McKay, *Vital Signs* (Westchester, IL: Crossway, 1984), p. 11ff.

2. Ibid., p. 11.

3. Ibid.

4. Ibid., pp. 13-14.

5. *Intercessors for America Newsletter* (April, 1986), Vol. 13, No. 4, p. 4.

6. James Robison, *Attack on the Family* (Wheaton, IL:

Tyndale House, 1980), p. 13.

7. Joann Ellison Rodgers, "A Life Without Father," *Parade Magazine* (May 12, 1985), p. 17.

8. 1 Corinthians 13:8.

9. We do not want to endorse the tendency we see today against hard work. You need to work hard. But, your wife must know she comes before your work and social life. Without that assurance, your marriage will not be vital and God's best.

10. Deuteronomy 5:16; Ephesians 6:2.

Chapter 11

1. "Morality," *U.S. News & World Report* (December 9, 1985), p. 52.

2. Don Baker, "The Least of These My Neighbors," *Leadership 100* (November/December 1982), pp. 11-12.

3. Interview with Jim Spinks (February, 1985).

4. Tim LaHaye, *The Battle for the Mind* (Old Tappan, NJ: Fleming H. Revell, 1980), pp. 203-04.

Chapter 12

1. Frederick Williams, *The Communications Revolution* (New York: New American Library, 1982), p. 15.

2. Karen Scalf Linamen, "What is Your Family Watching?" *Focus on the Family* (March 1985), p. 3.

3. Alvin P. Sanoff interview with Neil Postman, "TV

'Has Culture by the Throat,'" *U.S. News & World Report* (December 23, 1985), pp. 58-59.

4. S. Robert Lichter, Stanley Rothman, "Media and Business Elites," *Public Opinion* (October/November, 1981).

5. Linamen, "Family," p. 3.

6. Undated fund-raising letter from Norman Lear.

7. Carol Innerst, "More Journalism Schools Are Offering Courses in Ethics," *The Washington Times* (December 11, 1984), p. 5A.

8. Linamen, "Family," p. 3.

9. National Federation for Decency, P.O. Box 2440, Tupelo, MS 38803.

10. Quotes taken from interview with John Jones (October 13, 1984).

11. In 1985, CBN's "National Operation Blessing" helped over 8.5 million people. They dispersed over $11.5 million directly in food and goods and had another $37.5 million from matching funds and gifts in kind that were also dispersed.

Chapter 13

1. Interview with Bruce Wilkinson (January 28, 1985).

2. Thomas J. Peters, and Robert H. Waterman, Jr., *In Search of Excellence* (New York: Warner, 1982), p. 255.

3. Interview with John Boyer (February 15, 1985).

4. Matthew 22:39; 7:12.

5. John 13:35.

6. Interview with Chuck Stair (May 17, 1985).

7. The Hebrew word translated "gracious" gives the picture of a superior bending over or bowing to an inferior. This word, as an adjective, is always used in reference to God. It depicts a heartfelt response by someone who has something to give to one who has a need. R. Laird Harris, Gleason L. Archer, Jr., and Bruce K. Waltke, *Theological Wordbook of the Old Testament* (Chicago: Moody, 1980), pp. 302-4.

8. Interview with Chris White (February 16, 1985).

9. Boyer interview (February 15, 1985).

10. Stair interview (May 17, 1985).

11. Luke 12:15; Acts 20:35.

12. *Worldwide Challenge* (November/December, 1985), pp. 69-74.

13. Matthew 6:33.

Chapter 14

1. Report and Interview with George Gallup on "The 700 Club" (November, 1984).

2. Thomas Jefferson, *The Writings of Thomas Jefferson* (1892, 1899), comp. Paul Leicester Ford, Vol. 1, p. 447; cited by John Eidsmoe in *The Christian Legal Advisor* (Milford, MI: Mott Media, 1984), p. 392.

3. Harold O. J. Brown, *The Reconstruction of the Repub-*

lic (New Rochelle, NY: Arlington House, 1977), p. 19.

4. *The Los Angeles Times* (January 24, 1986), Part I, p. 6.

5. *The Los Angeles Times* (March 29, 1986), Part I-A, p. 1.

6. Proverbs 16:32; Ecclesiastes 12:13,14; Colossians 3:23,24.

7. Deuteronomy 6:5-9; Proverbs 1:8,9; Ephesians 6:4.

8. Matthew 16:18,19; 18:15-20; 1 Timothy 3:1-7; Hebrews 13:7,17; 1 Peter 5:2-4.

9. John 19:10, 11; Romans 13:1-4.

10. Romans 13:1-7; 1 Timothy 2:1-4.

11. "The Bible and Senator Armstrong," *Worldwide Challenge* (November/December, 1983), p. 43.

12. Jules Archer, *How Elections Work in America: Winners and Losers* (New York: Harcourt Brace Jovanovich, 1984), p. 176.

13. Ibid., p. 177.

14. Ibid., p. 204.

15. Proverbs 11:11 (The Living Bible).

16. John Rees, "Morton Blackwell," *The Review of the News* (October 3, 1984), p. 39.

17. Ibid.

18. Interview with Dr. Steven F. Hotze (January 31, 1985).

Chapter 15

1. Timothy J. Beals, "A Judge's Appeal for Justice," *Moody Monthly* (December, 1983), pp. 59-60.

2. Ibid., p. 60.

3. Ibid.

4. Deuteronomy 1:16,17.

5. Peggy Lamson, *Roger Baldwin: Founder of the American Civil Liberties Union* (Boston: Houghton Mifflin, 1976), p. 1920.

6. Interview with John Whitehead (January 28, 1985).

7. Ibid.

8. Summary taken from *The Rutherford Institute* newsletter (January/February, 1985), Vol. 2, No. 1, p. 7.

9. Whitehead interview.

10. John Whitehead, *Second American Revolution* (Elgin, IL: David C. Cook, 1982), Chapter 4: "Law Without An Anchor."

Chapter 16

1. *Newsweek* (May 9, 1983), p. 50.

2. James McKeen Cattell, *School and Society* (January 30, 1915), Vol. 1, No. 5, p. 179; cited by Samuel L. Blumenfeld, *N.E.A.: Trojan Horse in American Education* (Boise: The Paradigm Co., 1984), p. 102.

3. Ibid.

4. *TIME* (May 9, 1983), p. 62.

5. *Newsweek* (May 9, 1983), p. 50.

6. Blumenfeld, *N.E.A.: Trojan Horse*, pp. 1-5.

7. Samuel L. Blumenfeld, *Is Public Education Necessary?* (Old Greenwich, Conn.: The Devin-Adair Co., 1981), pp. 101-02.

8. Interview with Samuel L. Blumenfeld, by John Rees in *The Review of the News* (January 2, 1985), pp. 35-40.

9. Carl R. Rogers, "A Plan for Self-Directed Change in an Educational System," *Educational Leadership* (May, 1967), p. 717; cited by Barbara M. Morris, *Change Agents in the Schools*, (Upland, CA: The Barbara M. Morris Report, 1979), p. 49.

10. William D. Hedges and Marian L. Martinello, "What the Schools Might Do: Some Alternatives for the Here and Now," Louise M. Berman and James A. Roderick, editors, *Feeling, Valuing, and the Art of Growing* (Washington, DC: Association for Supervision and Curriculum Development, 1977), p. 231; cited by Barbara M. Morris in *Change Agents*, pp. 23-24.

11. Deuteronomy 6:7.

12. Proverbs 22:6.

13. Psalm 111:10.

14. Deuteronomy 6:4-9; Psalm 78:5-8; Ephesians 6:4.

15. For excellent introduction to Home Education see books by Raymond and Dorothy Moore, such as *Home*

Grown Kids(Waco: Word, 1981).

16. Interview with Steve Wyper (February 10, 1985).

17. John W. Whitehead, *The Freedom of Religious Expression in the Public High Schools* (Westchester, IL: Crossway, 1983), p. 34.

18. Ibid.

19. Ann Landers column, (March 24, 1986).

20. Alvin Sanoff interview with Steven Muller, "Universities Are Turning Out Highly Skilled Barbarians," *U.S. News and World Report* (November 10, 1980), pp. 57-58.

Chapter 17

1. *The World Almanac and Book of Facts, 1984,* p. 109.

2. Marvin Stone, "Movies and TV—Good or Bad?" *U.S. News and World Report* (October 31, 1983), p. 92.

3. "Can Any Good Thing Come Out of Hollywood?" An interview with producer Ken Wales, *Christianity Today* (September 21, 1984), p. 21.

4. Greg Brezina, "Almost All I Got for Christmas was Soft-Porn," *Communicating Christian Concepts, Inc.* newsletter, (January, 1984).

5. See Chapter Resource list of athletic ministry teams.

Chapter 18

1. Henry M. Morris, *Men of Science—Men of God* (San Diego: Creation-Life, 1982), p. 105.

2. Ibid., p. 71.

3. Ibid., pp. 105-106.

4. Fred Hoyle, *The Intelligent Universe: A New View of Creation and Evolution* (New York: Holt, Rinehart and Winston, 1983), pp. 11-12.

5. Roy Abraham Varghese, editor, *The Intellectuals Speak Out About God* (Chicago: Regnery Gateway, 1984), p. xxvi.

6. Ibid., p. 32.

7. "A Conversation with Sir John Eccles," *U.S. News and World Report* (December 10, 1984), p. 80.

8. Genesis 1:28.

Bibliography

The books selected for the bibliography, following each chapter, are the best sources for help the authors are aware of; we do not necessarily endorse all the contents or the positions of the books' authors. An attempt has been made to classify each book as to its content level. Those of an introductory nature are labeled (I) and those of a more advanced or in-depth nature are labeled (A).

We have placed double asterisks (**) beside the titles of those books considered to be the best in basic and introductory nature to help you begin to develop a biblical world and life view. We have placed a single askerisk (*) beside those titles recommended for the next level of reading and involvement.

CHAPTER 2:

Books recommended for further study:

**1. *The Stealing of America*
John W. Whitehead
Westchester, IL: Crossway, 1983.

Summarizes the great American legal tragedy and traces its decay. Includes insightful analysis in comparing Nazi Germany to present-day America. (A)

2. *The Rebirth of America*
   Nancy Leigh DeMoss, ed.
   n.p.: Arthur S. DeMoss Foundation, 1986.

   Available from:
   America
   P.O. Box 1000
   Valley Forge, PA 19481

Laid out beautifully on the order of *Ideals* magazine this book is divided into three sections: (1) "America Yesterday: A Nation Established," covers our heritage; (2) "America Today: A Nation Adrift," covers the breakdown of our society; and (3) "America Tomorrow: A Nation Reborn," a challenge to rediscover what initially made our nation great. (I)

3. *The Christian Voice Guide: Strategies for Reclaiming America*
   Editor-in-chief Colonel V. Doner
   Pacific Grove, CA: Renod Productions, 1984.

   Available from:
   Alive and Free
   131 Stony Circle, Suite 750-C
   Santa Rosa, CA 95401

A field manual about Christian activism, under providence of God, to give guidance to concerned Christian Americans who wish to make their influence felt, and who are willing to stand up and make their voices heard. (I)

4. *Together We Can Deal With Life in the '80s*
   Ron Jenson with Chuck MacDonald

San Bernardino, CA: Here's Life, 1982.

A documentation of the breakdown of American society and the role humanism is playing before an apathetic church. Clear-cut steps to spiritual revolution are given. (I)

5. *The Light and the Glory*
   Peter Marshall, Jr. and David Manuel, Jr.
   Old Tappan, NJ: Fleming H. Revell, 1977.

Traces the providential hand of God in the discovery, establishment, and guiding of our nation. Surfaces little-known or forgotten facts about American history. (I)

6. *Exploding the Myths That Could Destroy America*
   Erwin Lutzer
   Chicago: Moody, 1986.

This book is an up-to-date analysis of America's present spiritual and social condition and provides ammunition on how Christians can get involved to help change the world with an optimistic note that we can win the war. (I)

7. *If the Foundations Be Destroyed*
   James T. Draper and Forrest E. Watson
   Nashville, TN: Thomas Nelson, 1984

Gives an overview of the biblical foundations of the American republic. This book maintains that Americans will lose the blessings of liberty unless we restore the biblical heritage of our nation. (A)

8. *Vital Signs: Emerging Social Trends and the Future of American Christianity* George Barna and William Paul McKay
   Westchester, IL: Crossway, 1984

This is a book about the future. Our country has entered a period of radical social change. This book evaluates how

Christians are responding to the changes that have already started to reshape the contours of American society. (A)

9. *Before It's Too Late*
   David Jeremiah
   Nashville: Thomas Nelson, 1982.

This book discusses issues of personal and national concern to Christians. With the traditional values and principles that secured this country's greatness being ignored, David Jeremiah gives detailed biblical solutions for immediate action. (I)

10. *Theological Interpretation of American History*, rev. ed.
    C. Gregg Singer
    Nutley, NJ: Presbyterian and Reformed, 1981.

Shows the ideologies that shaped American thinking from biblical Christianity to New Deal Socialism. (A)

Action and assistance sources:

1. Plymouth Rock Foundation
   P.O. Box 425
   Marlborough, NH 03455

Book: *One Nation Under God*. By Rus Walton. Christian idea of government and God's laws of freedom. Also request newsletter, which covers topics related to the Christian world view, with a biblical analysis.

2. American Christian Task Force
   P.O. Box 1895
   Washington, DC 20013

Seeks to keep Christians informed of issues and activities of special interest in government. Request a publications list.

3. Foundation for Christian Self-Government
   (also known as Mayflower Institute)
   P.O. Box 1087
   Thousand Oaks, CA 91360

Book: *The American Covenant: The Untold Story.* An introduction to America's Christian history, and a workbook for Verna Hall's books below. Seminars on America's Christian history. Request a seminar schedule.

4. Foundation for American Christian Education
   P.O. Box 27035
   San Francisco, CA 94127

Books: *The Christian History of the American Revolution: Consider and Ponder.* Compiled by Verna Hall. A compilation of historical documents on the Revolution taken from diaries, sermons, and other extracts.

The Christian History of the Constitution of the United States of America: Christian Self-Government With Union. Compiled by Verna Hall. A compilation of documents showing the Christian influence in the shaping of our Constitution.

5. Student Action Coalition
   P.O. Box 19458
   Denver, CO 80219

Assistance provided for organizing students to bring forth Divine Law for society, thereby restoring the strength of our nation.

CHAPTER 3

Books recommended for further study:

*1. *Does Inerrancy Matter?*
James Montgomery Boice

Order booklet from:
International Council on Biblical Inerrancy
P.O. Box 12361
Oakland, CA 94661

Addresses the inerrancy issue and its importance. Succinct and to the point. (A)

2. *How Should We Then Live?*
Francis Schaeffer
Westchester, IL: Crossway, 1983.

A comprehensive view of the decline of Western thought and culture due to the abandonment of Judeo-Christian ideals for secularism and statism. (A)

3. *The Foundation of Biblical Authority*
Ed. James Montgomery Boice

Order from:
International Council on Biblical Inerrancy
P.O. Box 12361
Oakland, CA 94661

Results of the International Council on Biblical Inerrancy. Each chapter addresses a particular issue related to biblical authority. (A)

4. *Foundations of Christian Scholarship*
Ed. Gary North
Vallecito, CA: Ross House, 1976.

Chapters explore the implications of biblical faith for a variety of disciplines. (A)

5. *What In the World Is Real?*
Compiled by L'Abri Fellowship

Champaign, IL: Communication Institute, 1982.

Order from:
Communication Institute
P.O. Box 612
Champaign, IL 61820

Articles written by Francis and Edith Schaeffer and various L'Abri associates designed to take the question, *What in the World is Real?* into a variety of life's issues with the desire to challenge the superficial values characteristic of the society in which we live. These articles are offered to expose these superficial values in the firm belief that God uses His truth to change lives. (A)

6. *Unconditional Surrender: God's Program for Victory* 2nd ed.
   Gary North
   Tyler, TX: Geneva Divinity School, 1983.

Sections I and II give an excellent biblical world view blueprint for individual and society. Section III is eschatological in nature and debatable. (I)

7. *The Central Significance of Culture*
   Francis Nigel Lee
   Nutley, NJ: Presbyterian and Reformed, 1976 (out of print)

Analyzes the Christian's comprehensive responsibility under God to cultivate the world over which God has made us stewards. (A)

8. *Creation Regained: Biblical Basis for a Reformational World View*
   Albert M. Wolters
   Grand Rapids, MI: Eerdmans, 1985.

Wolters explains why the two-realms (sacred and secular) theory of Christian involvement reduced Christian action to the area of personal piety of the inner soul and church work and led to the secularization of Western culture. Separation from the world is to be ethical, a separation from sin, not geographical. (A)

9. *The Secret Kingdom*
Pat Robertson
Nashville: Thomas Nelson, 1982.

Deals with the "laws of the kingdom," principles by which each Christian is to function in society as an out-working of his religious duty under God. (I)

10. *Christianity as a Life-System: The Witness of a World View*
Abraham Kuyper (Former Prime Minister of The Netherlands)

Order from:
Christian Studies Center
P.O. Box 11110
Memphis, TN 38111

Reprint of the Stone Lectures delivered at Princeton Theological Seminary in 1898 focusing attention on the fundamental problem facing Christianity in Europe and America: the secularization of church and society. (A)

Action and assistance sources:

1. Intercessors for America
P.O. Box 1289
Elyria, OH 44036

An organization committed to seeing Christians take seriously the directive in 2 Chronicles 7:14. Their objectives: to inform, so Christians can pray intelligently and specifically; to encourage through reporting the ways God is active in our behalf; to instruct on the nature of spiritual warfare; and to inspire purposeful, Spirit-directed involvement in activites which further the cause of righteousness.

2. Probe Ministries
   1900 Firman Dr., Suite 100
   Richardson, TX 75081

A ministry dedicated to confronting the issues on college and university campuses through forums and publications. Request book and publications list.

3. Center for Conservative Alternatives
   Hillsdale College
   Hillsdale, MI 49242

Request "Imprimis," a publication on various issues addressed by noted conservative scholars and statesmen, not necessarily Christian.

4. Rockford Institute
   934 N. Main Street
   Rockford, IL 61103

Conservative, but not necessarily Christian, think tank that publishes articles covering a wide variety of national public policy issues. Articles tend to be on a more academic level.

CHAPTER 4

Books recommended for further study:

*1. *Comparing World Views, Vol. I of World View Series.*

   Order from:
   Public Policy Resource Center
   International Christian Graduate University

P.O. Box 50015
San Bernardino, CA 92412

A comparison of biblical, secular humanistic, and cosmic humanistic world views in handy chart form for quick reference. (A)

**2.   *The Battle for the Mind*
       Tim LaHaye
       Old Tappan, NJ: Fleming H. Revell, 1980.

LaHaye seeks to alert Christians to the two basic lines of reasoning that determine the morals, values, life-style and activities of mankind. Basically we are guided by either man's wisdom (humanism) or God's wisdom (the Bible). He challenges Christians to stand up and be counted. (I)

 *3.   *Biblical Principles: Concerning Issues of Importance to Godly Christians*
       Plymouth, MA: Plymouth Rock Foundation, 1984.

A catalog of issues addressed from a biblical perspective. A handy reference tool for the average layman to get a concise understanding of what the Bible has to say about a particular issue ranging from "Abortion" to "Women and 'Equal Rights.'" (I)

 *4.   *SCP Journal* (Spiritual Counterfeits Project)
       Winter 1981-82, Vol. 5, No. 1
       "Empowering the Self: A Look at the Human Potential Movement"

       Order from:
       Spiritual Counterfeits Project
       P.O. Box 4308
       Berkeley, CA 94704

A collection of articles that includes one of the first landmark articles to identify the emergence of cosmic humanism, which seeks to fill the spiritual void of secular humanism. This important journal identifies the fragmentation our society has experienced because of our worship of ideological pluralism. The human potential movement and the field of psychology, viz., Freud, Jung, Skinner, Rogers and Maslow, are identified as two fertile areas for developing cosmic humanism as a counterfeit answer to man's and society's problems. (A)

5. *The Essentials of a Christian World View*

Order from:
Coalition on Revival
89 Pioneer Way
Mountain View, CA 94041

Affirmation and denial statements of the essentials of what evangelical Christians believe. (I)

6. *The Spirit of Truth and the Spirit of Error*
Keith L. Brooks, Comp.
Chicago: Moody, 1976 rev. ed.

Handy chart of seven fundamental Christian doctrines comparing what the Word of God says and what six cults (Christian Science, Spiritualism, Jehovah's Witnesses, Armstrongism, Mormonism, and Eastern Mysticism) have to say on each doctrine. Well documented and in a fold-out form. (Not a book.) (I)

7. *The Universe Next Door*
James Sire
Downers Grove, IL: InterVarsity, 1977.

A catalog of world views. Develops definitions for a Christian world view and competing naturalistic world views. (A)

8. *Perspectives: Understanding and Evaluating Today's World Views*

Norman L. Geisler and William Watkins
San Bernardino, CA: Here's Life, 1984.

A comprehensive catalog of seven major world views. (A)

9. *Exposing New Age Philosophies*
    Barbara Hanna and Janet Hoover

    Order from:
    Pro-Family Forum
    P.O.Box 8907
    Ft. Worth, TX 76112

Outlines the essentials of the New Age Movement and illustrates with examples how the New Age philosophy has infiltrated various aspects of our society. (I)

10. *What Is Secular Humanism?*
     James Hitchcock
     Ann Arbor, MI: Servant, 1982.

This book probes the origins of the humanist movement, its momentum through history, its present impact on Western civilization, and its probable future course. Hitchcock is professor of history at St. Louis University. (A)

11. *Humanism In the Light of Holy Scripture*
     Homer Duncan
     Lubbock, TX: Missionary Crusader, 1981.

     Order from:
     Missionary Crusader
     4606 Avenue H
     Lubbock, TX 79404

Companion volume to *Secular Humanism: The Most Dangerous Religion in America*. This is an excellent introduction to secular humanism with many documented cases of humanistic influence in our nation. The author contrasts humanistic philosophy of life with God's view as revealed in Scripture. (I)

12. *Unmasking the New Age*
    Douglas R. Groothuis
    Downers Grove, IL: InterVarsity, 1986.

Exposes the philosophy of the New Age Movement and lists its manifestations in different areas of life. (I)

13. *The Holistic Healers: A Christian Perspective on New Age Health Care*
    Paul C. Reisser, M.D., Teri K. Reisser, and John Weldon Downers Grove, IL: InterVarsity, 1983.

Examines the roots of the holistic health movement and its therapies, including acupuncture, psychic healing and therapeutic touch. Exposes the Eastern mysticism and occultism which undergirds much of the movement. Looks at health from a biblical perspective. (A).

14. *New Age Globalism*
    Dr. H. Edward Rowe
    Herndon, VA: Growth, 1985

Describes the humanist agenda for a one-world government controlled by an international elite. It also documents how we are being prepared for this through avenues such as the classroom and the media. (A)

Action and assistance sources:

1. Public Policy Resource Center
   International Christian Graduate University
   P.O. Box 50015
   San Bernardino, CA 92412

Publishes a newsletter on social issues from a biblical world view. "Think tank" and resource center of the uni-

versity dedicated to providing assistance in developing
biblical thinking and action on numerous issues. Ask for
their recommended reading and resource lists and information packets on social, moral and spiritual warfare
issues.

2. Here's Life Publishers
   P.O. Box 1576
   San Bernardino, CA 92402-1576

Especially helpful is *Handbook of Today's Religions* by
Josh McDowell and Don Stewart. A popular reference
book on cults, the occult, secular and non-Christian religions. Also request a list of publications and tapes.

3. American Vision
   P.O. Box 720515
   Atlanta, GA 30328

A biblical world view ministry publishing "Insight" newsletter, a "God and Government" workbook series, and
various other publications.

4. Spiritual Counterfeits Project
   P.O. Box 4308
   Berkeley, CA 94704

Request a catalog of tapes and materials dealing with the
cults, the occult, and non-Christian religions. Also publishes *SCP Journal*, which seeks to biblically critique
current religious groups, philosophies and individuals.

5. Christian Activist
   P.O. Box 909
   Los Gatos, CA 95031

A Franky Schaeffer production newspaper designed to
keep readers updated on current events, pro-life issues,
the media, and analysis of Western society.

6. Chalcedon Report
   P.O. Box 158
   Vallecito, CA 95251

Publishes a monthly publication that deals with contemporary culture in light of biblical law.

7. Christian Information Bureau
   6102 E. Mockingbird, #231
   Dallas, TX 75214

Seeks to equip Christians with information to correlate world biblical prophecy. Request catalog of helps for spiritual discernment.

8. Southwest Radio Church
   P.O. Box 1144
   Oklahoma City, OK 73101

A daily conservative, non-denominational, evangelical radio ministry that addresses a variety of world-view issues of practical concern to pastors and laymen. Request a list of publications and tapes.

9. "New Age: Pathway to Paradise"
   (A set of three video cassettes)

   Distributed by:
   TV 38/WCFC
   1 N. Wacker Dr., Suite 1100
   Chicago, IL 60606
   (312) 977-3838

According to many New Age researchers around the nation, this is the best series ever done on the New Age influence in America.

10. "Gods of the New Age"
    (16mm film or video cassette)
    Rivershield Film Ltd. Production

Distributed by:
New Horizons Film Lab.
2218 W. Olive Ave.
Burbank, CA 91506

Documentary tracing the New Age Movement in the U.S.
to its Eastern roots in Indian Hinduism. Very revealing
and sobering.

11. "Revival of Evil"
     New Liberty Films
     (Video cassette narrated by Dave Hunt)

     Distributed by:
     Christian Films
     P.O. Box 2305
     La Habra, CA 90631
     (213) 691-0967 or (714) 871-5670

Documentary demonstrating the amount of overt and
casual occultism and Satan worship in the U.S. today.

CHAPTER 5

        Books recommended for further study:

**1. *Invisible War: Panorama of the Continuing Conflict
      Between Good and Evil*
      Donald Grey Barnhouse
      Grand Rapids, MI: Zondervan, 1965.

An examination of the spiritual conflict between good
and evil, beginning before recorded time and tracing the
development to the present time. Clearly reveals, from
Scripture, the winning side. (A)

**2. *Peace, Prosperity and the Coming Holocaust*
      Dave Hunt

Eugene, OR: Harvest House, 1983.

A good introduction to the "New Age Movement," which is the name for groups that promote the philosophies of cosmic humanism. (I)

*3. *Idols for Destruction*
Herbert Schlossberg
Nashville: Thomas Nelson, 1983.

An analysis of the difference between a Christian world view and a secular, anti-Christian world view in a number of areas and on a wide range of issues. (A)

4. *The Adversary: The Christian Versus Demon Authority*
Mark I. Bubeck
Chicago: Moody, 1975.

Approaches the subject of spiritual warfare from a practical viewpoint. (I)

5. *The Strategy of Satan*
Warren W. Wiersbe
Wheaton, IL: Tyndale House, 1983.

A manual of arms for the Christian soldier who is on the battlefield and wants to know how to win. Basic biblical instruction is given on the strategies of the devil.(I)

6. *Your Adversary the Devil*
J. Dwight Pentecost
Grand Rapids: Zondervan, 1969.

The author purposes to help us understand that large body of Scripture that reveals to us the person and work of the one with whom we, as Christians, are at war. The book is a systematic approach to the subject of spiritual warfare. (A)

7. *Christianity and Civilization, Vol. III: The Tactics of Christian Resistance*
Ed. Gary North
Tyler, TX: Geneva Divinity School Press, 1983.

A symposium on Christian resistance, scholarly, non-technical and aimed at the layman. Each chapter by a different author addresses the subject of Christian resistance. (A)

Action and assistance sources:

(See those listed for chapter four.)

CHAPTER 6

Books recommended for further study:

1. *Love Letter to America*
Tomas Schuman
Los Angeles: Almanac Panorama, 1984.

Order from:
Almanac
501 S. Fairfax Ave., Suite 206
Los Angeles, CA 90036

By a former KGB journalist who defected to the U.S.; appeals to Americans to wake up—we are at war! He reveals how the Communists are winning through ideological subversion though most Americans don't even realize it. (I)

2. *How Democracies Perish*
Jean-Francois Revel
New York: Doubleday, 1984.

Can a free society survive against the pressures of totalitarianism? Revel, a French socialist and humanist, retreating from Marxism, suggests that the freedoms and values of democracy may be the seeds of its own destruction against an ideology that will trample what it perceives as inherent weaknesses. If democracy is to survive, it must stand against the evil and not compromise, or its doom is sealed. (A)

3. *Bad News for Modern Man: An Agenda for Christian Activism*
   Franky Schaeffer
   Westchester, IL: Crossway, 1984.

Exposes the infiltration of a secular world view in evangelicalism. A call to action and a practical agenda to stop the slide of our culture. (I)

4. *Judges: God's War Against Humanism*
   James B. Jordan
   Tyler, TX: Geneva Ministries, 1985.

The first of a planned series in the Trinity Biblical Commentaries. Written in non-technical language, yet designed for the serious student. Judges is a book about faith and single-mindedness as Israel confronts the secular humanism of its day in the form of Baalism. Jordan feels Judges has many practical lessons to teach the church today. (A)

5. *Fire in the Minds of Men*
   James H. Billington
   New York: Basic Books, 1980.

An important work recognizing revolution, in the modern sense, as an expression of religious faith. This massive study demonstrates the anti-Christian and pseudo-Christian character of worldly revolutionary ideology. Billington asserts that revolutionary faith did not originate in the critical rationalism of the French Enlightenment, but earlier in 18th century Prussian Germany, which experienced a revival of occult romanticism of secret societies which syncretized Christian symbolism and pagan mysticism. It is also interesting to note that the Unitarians, who introduced compulsory attendance in state-controlled public schools in America, imported many of their ideas from the Prussian public school system. (A)

6. *Backward Christian Soldiers*
   Gary North
   Tyler, TX: Institute for Christian Economics, 1984.

This book includes an excellent list of detailed, practical strategies for reclaiming our culture for Christ. Although your eschatology may differ from North's, the vision of Christ's claims needs to be extended to all of life, which he proposes in *Backward Christian Soldiers*. (A)

7. *The Generation That Knew Not Josef*
   Lloyd Billingsley
   Portland, OR: Multnomah, 1985.

Billingsley admonishes Christians to learn the lessons of history. Historically ignorant Christians are easy prey for the utopian promises of the Marxist-Leninist prophets. He gives us a sampling of Christians in our century who have been taken in by the utopian visionaries, as well as a sampling of others who have seen through the false prophets. Written with wit and historical insight. (A)

8. *Suicide of the West*
   James Burnham
   Chicago: Regnery, 1985.

A classic, back in print, that exposes liberalism, revealing its true nature, and giving the inside thinking and reasoning for the failure of liberalism. Burnham offers his "39 Articles of Liberalism," which can be used to determine your "ideological quotient." (A)

CHAPTER 7

Books recommended for further study:

*1. *The Christian Mind*
Harry Blamires
Ann Arbor, MI: Servant, 1963.

Develops the thesis that Christians have surrendered their minds to secular explanations of reality. The second part examines what presuppositions are needed in developing a Christian mind. (A)

2. *Every Thought Captive*
Richard L. Pratt, Jr.
Phillipsburg, NJ: Presbyterian and Reformed, 1979.

A study manual for the defense of Christian truth; a book aimed at training young people to be apologists. Written for the Christian high school student, it is a good introduction to how to think biblically. (I)

3. *Biblical Philosophy of History*
R. J. Rushdoony
Phillipsburg, NJ: Presbyterian and Reformed, 1979.

Shows how the biblical doctrine of creation is the foundation for establishing a true understanding of history, as time, man, the universe and history are the product of a sovereign God from whom all things derive their meaning. (A)

4. *How to Read Slowly: A Christian Guide to Reading with the Mind*
James Sire
Downers Grove, IL: InterVarsity, 1978 (out of print).

A sequel to *The Universe Next Door* as the author explains how to discern an author's world view as reflected in his writing. (A)

5. *Win the Battle for Your Mind*
    Richard L. Strauss
    Wheaton, IL: Victor, 1980.

The author seeks to give biblical answers to such questions as: What does God say about the use of your mind? How should you think? How can you handle unacceptable thoughts? How should you properly program your mind? and other questions. Strauss has designed the book to be used in group study. (I)

Action and assistance sources:

1. Public Policy Resource Center
    International Christian Graduate University
    P.O. Box 50015
    San Bernardino, CA 92412

A department of the university which helps develop a biblical world view foundation for the university. Request a list of publications that would aid in developing a biblical world view.

2. The American Vision
    P.O. Box 720515
    Atlanta, GA 30328

Monthly newsletter called "Biblical World View Magazine" that develops a biblical world view of all areas of life.

3. Plymouth Rock Foundation
    P.O. Box 425
    Marlborough, NH 03455

"The Rock," a quarterly journal on the biblical alternative to humanism and socialism. Monthly "Letter From Plymouth Rock" and "Fac-Sheet."

4. Probe Ministries
   1900 Firman Dr., Suite 100
   Ricardson, TX 75081

A ministry dedicated to confronting the issues on college and university campuses through forums and publications. Request book and publications list.

5. Chalcedon Report
   P.O. Box 158, Vallecito, CA 95251

A monthly newsletter dealing with contemporary culture in light of Scripture.

6. Institute for Christian Economics
   P.O. Box 8000
   Tyler, TX 75711

A "think tank" which applies Scripture to economics and other areas. It publishes several newsletters, books and tapes.

CHAPTER 8:

Books recommended for further study:

1. *Handbook for Christian Maturity*
   Bill Bright
   San Bernardino, Calif.: Campus Crusade for Christ, 1981.

A series of Bible studies designed to cover the basics of the Christian life. (I)

2. *Independent Bible Study*

Irving L. Jensen
Chicago: Moody Press, 1970.

A basic guide to Bible study with emphasis on how to do a book chart.

3. *Layman's Guide to Interpreting the Bible*
   Walter A. Henrichsen
   Grand Rapids, Mich.: Zondervan Publishing Co. 1979.

A basic guide to Bible study. (I)

4. *Walk Thru the Bible*
   Bruce Wilkinson and Kenneth Boa
   Nashville: Thomas Nelson Publishers, 1983.

An excellent book covering in a survey form book charts and summary notes on each of the 66 books of the Bible. (I)

5. *The Thompson Chain Reference Bible* or
   The Open Bible.

Chain reference Bibles.

6. *Strong's Exhaustive Concordance*; or
   New American Standard Exhaustive Concordance of the Bible

Concordances of the Bible. (We recommend one that is keyed to Strong's numbering as this system of numbering is used by other Bible study aids and is a valuable assistance to the Bible student not familiar with the biblical languages.)

7. *Naves Topical Bible* or
   The New Compact Topical Bible

Topical Bibles.

8. *Macmillan Bible Atlas* or
   Baker's Bible Atlas

Atlases of Bible lands.

9. *The New Bible Dictionary* or
   Unger's Bible Dictionary

Bible dictionaries. (Recommend any recently published Bible dictionary. Also a must aid in Bible study.)

10. *Vine's Expository Dictionary of Old and New Testament Words*
    W. E. Vine
    Old Tappan, N.J.: Fleming H. Revell, 1981.

Allows the Bible student to gain an insight into the language of the New Testament, primarily, and some Old Testament words.

11. *Theological Wordbook of the Old Testament*
    ed. R. Laird Harris,
    Chicago: Moody Press, 1980.

Permits the Bible student to study Old Testament words by using a cross-referenced index of Strong's numbering system.

CHAPTER 9

Books recommended for further study:

*1. *Pursuit of Holiness*
    Jerry Bridges
    Colorado Springs: Navpress, 1978.

A book and Bible study designed to aid in the pursuit of holy living. (I)

2. *Handbook of Concepts for Living*
   Bill Bright
   San Bernardino, CA: Campus Crusade for Christ, 1981.

A collection of transferable concepts, written by Bill Bright, that are foundational to the Christian life. (I)

3. *Godliness Through Discipline*
   Jay E. Adams
   Grand Rapids: Baker, 1972.

Excellent, practical description on God's method of gaining victory in our personal lives through three principles of discipline (16-page booklet). (I)

4. *Dedication and Leadership*
   Douglas Hyde
   South Bend, IN: University of Notre Dame, 1966.

Insights on how the Communists successfully disciple their followers. Written by a former Communist. (I)

5. *A Time For Anger*
   Franky Schaeffer
   Westchester, IL: Good News Publishers, 1982.

Details the manner in which secular media and other news making and opinion making elites in this country have denigrated and sought to belittle Christianity. (I)

Action and assistance sources:

1. Campus Crusade For Christ
   Arrowhead Springs
   San Bernardino, CA 92414

Request list of ministries and publications that would be helpful for developing a revolutionary life-style.

2. Public Policy Resource Center
   International Christian Graduate University
   P.O. Box 50015
   San Bernardino, CA 92412

"Think tank" of the university dedicated to providing assistance in developing a biblical world view on numerous issues. A resource center for the advancement of biblical thinking and action.

3. International School of Theology
   P.O. Box 50015
   San Bernardino, CA 92412

Request list of publications that would be helpful for developing a revolutionary life-style.

4. Coalition on Revival
   89A Pioneer Way
   Mountain View, CA 94041

A steering committee of 100 national Christian leaders who have banded together for the purpose of helping to bring revival-renewal-reformation to Christianity. Dedicated to writing a Christian world-view document.

CHAPTER 10

Books recommended for further study:

1. *Battle for the Family*
   Tim LaHaye
   Old Tappan, NJ: Fleming H. Revell, 1983.

Identification of 15 major ways in which humanism infiltrates the home and family. Offers how to win the battle for your family. (I)

2. *Parents' Rights*
   John W. Whitehead
   Westchester, IL: Crossway, 1985.

Whitehead has written this book in hopes of making a positive comment on the problems facing parents, children, and families. (A)

3. *The Way Home*
    Mary Pride
    Westchester, IL: Crossway, 1985.

Franky Schaeffer says, "the best book ever written against feminism and for the home, family and child rearing. (I)

4. *The Christian Family*
    Larry Christenson
    Minneapolis: Bethany Fellowship, 1978.

Shows God's order for the family, and the family's relationship to Jesus Christ. (I)

5. *Spirit Controlled Family Living*
    Tim LaHaye
    Old Tappan, NJ: Fleming H. Revell, 1978.

Takes the concept of the Spirit-filled life and applies it specifically to each member of the family. Gives help on how to have victory over anger, depression, defeat, etc. (I)

6. *Nurturing Children in the Lord*
    Jack Fennema
    Grand Rapids: Baker, 1979 (reprint ed.)

The author begins with Scripture to determine patterns for the nurture that God wants for His children. Fennema has designed this book to be a study guide, not a handbook. He is primarily aiming at Christian pre-service or in-service teachers. He desires to provide an alternative to the thinking of the behaviorist and the humanist. (A)

7. *In Defense of the Family*
    Rita Kramer
    New York: Basic Books, 1983.

This is a compelling argument for the pro-family point of view vs. the anti-family propaganda put out by the feminist movement. The author stresses the idea of women putting their children and home as a "number one priority" ahead of career, money, and superficial prestige. (I)

8. *The Family: America's Hope*
   John A. Howard
   Rockford, IL: Rockford College Institute, 1979.

   Order from:
   The Rockford Institute
   934 N. Main Street
   Rockford, IL 61103

A collection of speeches presented at a national conference considering the role of the family in a free society. (A)

9. *What is a Family?*
   Edith Schaeffer
   Old Tappan, NJ: Fleming H. Revell, 1975.

Explores the many facets of a home as God meant it to be; many personal illustrations. (I)

Action and assistance sources:

1. Family Ministry
   Route 1, Box 14A
   Roland, AR 72135

Family ministry of Campus Crusade for Christ. Request a schedule of their outstanding Family Ministry Seminars and a list of other resources available throughout the U.S. and Canada.

2. Focus on the Family

P.O. Box 500
Arcadia, CA 91006

Ministry of psychologist Dr. James Dobson dedicated to addressing family issues.

3. Pro-Family Forum
    P.O. Box 8907
    Ft. Worth, TX 76112

A grassroots movement dedicated to promoting the family unit as the vital link in a continuing democracy. Seeks to inform people about harmful legislation.

4. Concerned Women for America
    122 "C" Street N.W., Suite 800
    Washington, D.C. 20001

Dedicated to informing women about the erosion of our historic Judeo-Christian moral standards and the insidious movements aimed at destroying the family.

5. Eagle Forum
    P.O. Box 618
    Alton, IL 62002

A national pro-family organization which believes Holy Scripture provides the best code of moral conduct yet devised and the family is the basic unit of society. Request publications list.

6. Institute in Basic Youth Conflicts
    Box 1
    Oak Brook, IL 60521

Ministry of Bill Gothard designed to help families apply basic scriptural principles to family life relationships and situations. Request seminar schedule and publications list.

CHAPTER 11

Books recommended for further study:

1. *The Great Evangelical Disaster*
   Francis Schaeffer
   Westchester, IL: Crossway, 1984.

Traces the how, where, and why of evangelicalism's compromise with secular humanism and liberalism from 1920's to present, and explains why evangelical leaders have been so silent and apathetic. (A)

2. *The Seduction of Christianity*
   Dave Hunt
   Eugene, OR: Harvest House, 1985.

An exposure of the subtle influence and deception of cosmic humanism (New Age thought) in evangelical churches today. (I)

3. *A Clear and Present Danger*
   William Stanmeyer
   Ann Arbor, MI: Servant, 1983.

Describes why we are confused by attempts to muzzle the Christian voice through talk of 'separation of church and state' and 'the establishment of religion.' (A)

4. *Christianity and Civilization, Vol. II: Theology of Christian Resistance*
   Ed. Gary North
   Tyler, TX: Geneva Divinity School, 1983.

Provides many workable plans for churches and Christian groups to resist unlawful government intrusions. Offers a concrete strategy for building a Christian culture. (A)

5. *Bringing in the Sheaves*

George Grant
Atlanta: American Vision, 1985.

Grant speaks not only from biblical knowledge but from practical experience as he says this book is a practical primer for families, churches and private enterprises who wish to begin erecting effective models of biblical charity all over the country. (A)

6. *No Other Foundation*
   Jeremy C. Jackson
   Westchester, IL: Crossway, 1980.

The author's purpose is to provide the reader with a history of the church which ventures to interpret the meaning of the past for our own day while keeping in touch with objective facts. Consequently, this is not just another book on church history, as the author approaches the subject as a social historian rather than a church historian. Can the church of today learn from her past? Jackson says, yes! (A)

7. *Let's Have a Reformation*
   Jay Grimstead
   Los Altos, CA: Reformation, 1982.

This concise, powerful book lays a solid biblical foundation for the massive overhaul that most of our present day churches desperately need. It is based on a sound accountability group strategy whose purpose is to help every pastor and member to grow toward Christian maturity. (I)

8. *The Gravedigger File: Sociological View of American Christianity*
   Os Guiness
   Downers Grove, IL: InterVarsity, 1983.

Written in story form, with the flavor of C.S. Lewis' *Screwtape Letters*, shows how the modern world squeezes the church into its mold, and brings into sharp focus the challenge to Christian discipleship in the late twentieth century. (A)

Action and assistance sources:

1. International School of Theology
    P.O. Box 50015
    San Bernardino, CA 92412

Committed to training future Christian leaders for the church, parachurch and other Christian organizations.

2. Here's Life America
    P.O. Box 26160
    Austin, TX 78755

Lay ministry of Campus Crusade for Christ which works through local churches.

3. Church Dynamics
    10658 Porto Court
    San Diego, CA 92124

Committed to the development of effective church leaders capable of mobilizing others to help fulfill the Great Commission of making disciples.

4. Coalition on Revival
    89A Pioneer Way
    Mountain View, CA 94041

A steering commitee of 100 national Christian leaders working toward a consensus conviction about where the Christian church should stand and what action it should take over the next ten years.

CHAPTER 12

Books recommended for further study:

1. *The Home Invaders*
   Donald E. Wildmon
   Wheaton, IL: Victor, 1985.

The author is formerly a pastor in Mississippi who became so provoked at the television media's indoctrination of humanist values that he founded the National Federation for Decency in 1977 to combat this onslaught. Now he has written a book to challenge Christians to join him in replacing the humanist view of man with the Christian view. Do not read it unless you are prepared to join Wildmon in his ongoing battle with the TV media invaders. (I)

2. *The Hidden Censors*
   Tim LaHaye
   Old Tappan, NJ: Fleming H. Revell, 1984.

LaHaye lifts the lid off the news and entertainment industry to reveal the amoral, socialistic, atheistic, and humanistic philosophies of those who have gained control of our nation's media. He provides vital information for us to effectively take action in shaking off humanism's strangle hold and restore decency and freedom of choice in the media. (I)

3. *Taming the TV Habit*
   Kevin Perotta
   Ann Arbor, MI: Servant Books, 1982.

A unique analysis of television's far-reaching effects on the Christian family. Offers parents practical help for controlling the use of TV in the home. (I)

4. *Panic Among the Philistines*
   Brian S. Griffin
   Chicago: Regnery Gateway, 1983.

An expose of the "artistic-media community" and its shabby amoral values. The author pops the media bubble and exposes the emperor in all his nakedness as never before. (A)

5. *Book Burning*
   Cal Thomas
   Westchester, IL: Crossway, 1983.

Answers the liberal charge that Christians are bigots and censors. Presents a positive case for a Christian view of free speech. (A)

6. *Target America*
   James L. Tyson
   Chicago: Regnery Gateway, 1981.

Exposes the history and current practice of "disinformation" and traces the influence of Communist propaganda and leftist ideology on U.S. media both past and present. (A)

Action and assistance sources:

1. Accuracy in Media
   777 14th Street, N.W.
   Washington, DC 20005

Publishes "AIM Report" twice monthly exposing serious media abuses.

2. National Federation for Decency
   P.O. Box 1434
   Alexandria, VA 22313

Serves as the hub group for the Coalition for Better Television, monotoring network TV programs and informing the Christian community which sponsors rate highest in sponsoring sex, violent, and profane programs.

3.   Morality in Media
     475 Riverside Dr.
     New York, NY 10115

Works to stop the traffic in pornography constitutionally
by informing parents and community leaders. Operates
as a clearing house, researching, collecting, and dis-
seminating information on the problems of obscenity.

CHAPTER 13

Books recommended for further study:

1.   *Free Enterprise*
     Harold Lindsell
     Wheaton, IL: Tyndale House, 1982.

Develops the biblical concept of private property and
shows its applicability for today. Also shows that
socialism is contrary to the commandment "Thou shalt
not steal." (A)

2.   *Your Finances in Changing Times*
     Larry Burkett
     Chicago: Moody, 1975.

Deals with present economy, biblical principles, and practical applications. (I)

3.   *Is Capitalism Christian?: Toward a Christian*
     Perspective on Economics
     Franky Schaeffer, editor
     Westchester, IL: Crossway, 1985.

This book answers the charge by Christian radicalism
that Western capitalism is fundamentally unjust and responsible for Third World poverty. Instead, it clearly
shows that hope for the Third World lies not in socialism

or communism but in the freedom and economic opportunity provided by democratic capitalism. (A)

4. *Bible Promises: Help and Hope for Your Finances*
   Dick Bruso
   San Bernardino, CA: Here's Life, 1985.

An alphabetical listing of major topics related to finances with appropriate Scriptures listed in the order in which they appear in the Bible. A helpful resource tool. (I)

5. *Managing Yourself*
   Stephen B. Douglass
   San Bernardino, CA: Here's Life, 1978.

This book provides practical help for Christians desiring to be more effective. It will help you learn how to find an overall direction in life, how to recognize each day's priorities, and how to enjoy and follow through on your priorities. The concepts presented are easy to understand and apply. (I)

6. *Your Wealth in God's World*
   John Jefferson Davis
   Phillipsburg, NJ: Presbyterian and Reformed, 1984.

Davis presents a biblically based position on the subjects of wealth, poverty, and the role of government in our nation's economic life. He purposes to chart a course between the "health and wealth gospel" and excessive state intervention in our society's ecomomic life. (A)

7. *The Pursuit of Excellence*
   Ted W. Engstrom
   Grand Rapids, MI: Zondervan, 1982

A challenge to shun mediocrity. (I)

8. *The Dominion Covenant: Genesis*

Gary North
Tyler, TX: Institute of Christian Economics, 1982.

The first of a projected multi-volume commentary based on the conviction that there is *revelational economics*. *Written to fill a void on the subject of biblical economics.* *(A)*

9. *A Christian Guide to Prosperity*
   Michael Fries & C. Holland Taylor
   with Ron Sunseri
   Oakland: Communications Research, 1984.

   Order from:
   Communication Research
   P.O. Box 11143
   Oakland, CA 94611

This is a sound, biblically based description of what is happening to the U.S. economy. It gives specific practical suggestions on what you must do to prepare for the coming day of reckoning for our inflated, indebted economy. It prepares you to provide for your family and be in a position to give to the Lord's work, the church, and to help the truly needy. (I)

10. *Stronger than Steel: The Wayne Alderson Story*
    R. C. Sproul
    New York: Harper & Row, 1983.

The story of a man who applied biblical principles in the work place and got fired and consequently began the ministry, Value of the Person. (I)

Action and assistance sources:

1. Executive Ministries of Campus Crusade for Christ
   4419 Cowan Rd., Suite 300
   Tucker, GA 30084

Ministry of Campus Crusade for Christ that works with business executives and professionals.

2. Institute for Christian Economics
   P.O. Box 8000
   Tyler, TX 75711

Founded on the conviction that biblical principles are the standard for economics, the ICE is dedicated to research and publication in the social sciences, especially economics. Request list of publications, newsletters, and position papers.

3. Christian Businessmen's Committee of U.S.A.
   P.O. Box 3380
   Chattanooga, TN 37404

Volunteer lay businessmen's group that encourages spiritual growth and outreach.

4. Value of the Person
   100 Ross Street
   Pittsburgh, PA 15219

A Wayne Alderson ministry that seeks to strike a balanced position between labor and management.

CHAPTER 14

Books recommended for further study:

1. *God and Government:*
   Vol. I: A Biblical and Historical Study, 1982.

Vol. II: Issues in Biblical Perspective, 1984.
Vol. III: The Restoration of the Republic, 1986.
Gary DeMar
Atlanta: American Vision Press, 1982

Order from:
American Vision
P.O. Box 720515
Atlanta, GA 30328.

Volume I: a ten-lesson, self-study workbook that traces
what the Bible teaches about types of government. (I)

Volume II: a ten-lesson, self-study workbook that traces
what the Bible teaches about world views and economics.
(I)

Volume III: a ten-lesson, self-study workbook that lays
the foundation for applying the Bible to society, nations,
and governments. (I)

2. *Biblical Principles: Concerning Issues of
    Importance to Godly Christians*
    Rus Walton
    Plymouth, MA: Plymouth Rock Foundation, 1984.

A catalog of issues addressed from a biblical perspective.
A handy reference tool for the average layman to get a
concise understanding of what the Bible has to say about
a paticular issue ranging from "Abortion" to "Women and
'Equal Rights.'" (I)

3. *One Nation Under God*
    Rus Walton
    Old Tappan, NJ: Fleming H. Revell, 1975

Chapters 1, 8, and 10 deal with the Christian idea of government, the controls of government, and taxation. (I)

4. *This Independent Republic*

Rousas J. Rushdoony
Fairfax, VA: Thoburn, 1978.

Rushdoony seeks to show that the roots of American history go deep extending all the way back to the origins of Christianity and on up through the Reformation. He feels it is time we recognize the religious presuppostions undergirding many non-religious aspects of colonial history. (A)

5. *The Reconstruction of the Republic: A Modern Theory of the State Under God and Its Political, Social, and Economic Structure.*
   Harold O. J. Brown
   Milford, MI: Mott Media, 1981.

Explodes the fallacy that religion and politics do not mix, pointing out that Christians took an active part in framing our laws on both the state and federal levels. (A)

6. *The Coercive Utopians*
   Rael and Erich Issac
   Chicago: Regnery Gateway, 1983.

This book exposes the *real* agenda of the social elite who are entrenched in the bureaucracy of mainline Protestant denominations; in the environmental, public interest, and peace movements; in the universities and a series of radical think tanks; all of whom are dedicated to ending our high standard of living and our democratic system.

7. *Separation of Church and State: Historical Fact and Current Fiction*
   Robert L. Cord
   New York: Lambeth, 1982.

Exhaustive historical documentaion of church and state relations in the U.S. (A)

8. *The Naked Public Square*
   Richard John Neuhaus

Grand Rapids: Eerdmans, 1984.

Neuhaus eloquently argues for the necessity to articulate a "public framework for moral reference." A rebuttal to the argument that politics and religion do not mix, the book challenges mainline Protestantism's social and political creeds which have replaced the true gospel. (A)

9. *A Time for Action*
    William E. Simon
    New York: McGraw-Hill, 1980.

A book on government and economic issues by the Secretary of the Treasury under the Nixion Administration.

10. *The Biblical Basis of Public Policy*
     Herbert W. Titus
     Virginia Beach, VA: National Perspective Institute, 1986.

How does God order the affairs of nations? Is there any scriptural justification for "separation of church and state?" Just what role should American believers play in the nation's political life? The answers to these thorny questions—and many others—are contained in this brief but powerful essay. (A)

Action and assistance sources:

1. Concerned Women for America
    122 "C" Street N.W., Suite 800
    Washington, DC 20001

Dedicated to informing women about the erosion of our historic Judeo-Christian moral standards and the insidious movements aimed at destroying the family.

2. Eagle Forum
    P.O. Box 618

Alton, IL 62002

Monthly newsletter by Phyllis Schlafly focusing attention on pro-family issues and issues of national concern.

3. The Free Congress Research and Education Foundation
721 2nd Street, N.E.
Washington, D.C. 20002

Analyzes U.S. House and Senate elections and studies current political trends which have national significance. Also focuses on trends affecting the stability and well-being of American family life. FCF publications, the "Family Protection Report" and "Family Policy Insight" are sent upon request to annual contributors of $25 or more for each publication.

4. American Coalition Task Force
P. O. Box 1895
Washington, D.C. 20013

Seeks to keep Christians informed of issues and activities of special interest in government. Request a publications list.

5. Heritage Foundation
214 Massachusetts Ave., N.E.
Washington, D.C. 20002

A leading public policy research institute providing research and study programs designed to make the voices of responsible conservatism heard in Washington, the United States, and the world.

CHAPTER 15

Books recommended for further study:

1. *The Second American Revolution*
   John W. Whitehead
   Elgin, IL: David C. Cook, 1982.

Traces the erosion of the American judicial system from its Judeo-Christian roots to its present state of erosion and confusion. Offers a strategy to restore constitutional government. (A)

2. *The Christian Legal Advisor*
   John Eidsmoe
   Milford, MI: Mott Media, 1984.

A complete and up-to-date guide to every Christian's rights and remedies under the law. A helpful statement of the Christian view of law. (A)

3. *Institutes of Biblical Law*
   Rousas J. Rushdoony
   Nutley, NJ: The Craig Press, 1972.

A detailed study of the Ten Commandments with other laws of the Bible catalogued under one or more of the Ten Commandments. (A)

4. *The Politics of the American Civil Liberties Union*
   William A. Donohue
   New Brunswick, NJ: Transaction, 1985

Donohue is associate professor and chairman of the Division of Social Sciences at La Roche College in Pittsburgh. He provides us with a critical analysis of the ACLU and liberalism in America in the 20th century. As a social scientist, he gives us a systematic analysis of both the ACLU and liberalism. The book is heavily documented. (A)

5. *The Criterion*
   Jerry Bergman
   Richfield, MN: Onesimus, 1984.

Order from:
Onesimus Publishing
6245 Newton Avenue South
Richfield, MN 55423

This book summarizes many shocking cases of academic discrimination gathered from the author's interview of more than 100 professors and students known to hold personal convictions that creation science is a better explanation of the scientific data than evolution. The discrimination fell into five basic categories which the author addresses. The author discovered that most of higher education champions and values academic freedom only for liberal and humanistic causes and not for biblical Christian and conservative causes. (A)

Action and assistance sources:

1. The Rutherford Institute
    P.O. Box 510
    Manassas, VA 22110

A Christ-centered legal action and training organization designed to reestablish the biblical basis of law that was once the foundation of our American system of law and government.

2. Blackstone Institute of Public Law and Policy
    P.O. Box 3358
    Abilene, TX 79604

Committed to combating the humanist assault on Judeo-Christian values as reflected in law, public policy, and legal theory.

3. Citizens for Decency Through Law, Inc.
    P.O. Box 35692
    Phoenix, AZ 85069-9981

Seeks to create awareness in the area of obscenity issues.

CHAPTER 16

Books recommended for further study:

1. *N.E.A.: Trojan Horse in American Education*
   Samuel Blumenfeld
   Boise: The Paradigm, 1984.

A sequel to *Is Public Education Necessary?* exposing the National Education Association's history and its design to become a political power with the aim of converting America into a humanistic, socialist society. (A)

2. *What Are They Teaching Our Children?*
   Mel and Norma Gabler
   Wheaton, IL: Victor, 1985.

Outlines different views of humanism and illustrates how these views are present in school textbooks, curriculum, classroom programs, and supplemental materials that are being used in public schools. (I)

3. *The Battle for Public Schools*
   Tim LaHaye
   Old Tappan, NJ: Fleming H. Revell, 1982.

An examination of the development and direction of public schools with emphasis on the apparent direction they are leading us as a nation. (I)

4. *Family Choice in Education: The New Imperative*
   Onalee McGraw

   Order booklet from:
   The Heritage Foundation
   214 Massachusets Ave., N.E.
   Washington, DC 20002

Drawing upon the writing of eminent scholars in the field of education, a case for family choice in education is presented. (I)

5. *Education for the Real World*
   Henry Morris
   San Diego: Creation Life, 1977.

Places education in its true biblical perspective, preparing people for fruitful lives in both time and eternity. (A)

6. *Intellectual Schizophrenia*
   Rousas J. Rushdoony
   Phillipsburg, NJ: Presbyterian and Reformed, 1961.

A penetrating look at America's current view of education contrasted with God's view. This book answers the question, "Why does education always reflect one's religion?" (A)

7. *Rebirth of Our Nation*
   Donald Howard
   Lewisville, TX: Accelerated Christian Education, 1979.

A sequel to the author's first book, *To Save a Nation*, this book reflects back on the 1970s, and identifies both the negative and the positive trends of that decade and looks forward to the 1980s with a new spirit of optimism. The author feels that God is intervening in American history with the rise of Christian schools all across the country to once again sow the principles of biblical theism in the hearts of our youth. (I)

8. *A Christian Approach to Education: Educational Theory and Application*, rev. ed.
   H. W. Bryne
   Milford, MI: Mott Media, 1977.

Outlines the differences between secular and Christian education. The integration of the Bible and specific subject areas is addressed in this volume. (A)

9. *Better Late than Early: A New Approach to Your Child's Education*
   Raymond S. & Dorthy N. Moore
   New York: Reader's Digest

   Order from:
   Hewitt Research Foundation
   36211 S.E. Sunset View
   Washougal, WA 98671

A well-documentated case, based on multi-discipline research, against the movement toward earlier schooling, showing that later entrance into formal academic training is better. (A)

10. *Child Abuse in the Classroom*
    Edited by Phyllis Schlafly
    Alton, IL: Pere Marquette, 1984.

Selected excerpts from the Official Transcript of Proceedings before the United States Department of Education in the matter of the Proposed Regulations to Implement the Protection of Pupil Rights Amendment, or better known as the "Hatch Amendment." (A)

Action and assistance sources:

1. Christian Leadership
   9502 Webb's Chapel Road, Suite 100
   Dallas, TX 75220

Campus Crusade for Christ Minsitry to reach faculty and administration on the college campus.

2. Educational Research Analysts
   P.O. Box 7518
   Longview, TX 75607

Specializing in evaluation of textbooks, and a clearing house of resources.

3. Accuracy In Academia
   1275 "K" St., N.W.
   Washington, DC 20005

Publishers of "The Campus Report," which reports on the use of the university classroom as a platform for propaganda and discrimination against conservative and/or Christian faculty, staff and students.

4. National Association of Christian Educators
   P.O. Box 3200
   Costa Mesa, CA 92628

An organization of Christian professional educators committed to excellence in both academics, moral and spiritual values in the public schools.

5. Christian Home Schools
   8731 N.W. Everett Street
   Portland, OR 97220

"Teaching Home," an important newsletter, presents a broad scope of information on a national level.

6. Association of Christian Schools International
   P.O. Box 4097
   Whittier, CA 90631

A service organization serving Christian schools across the nation and around the world.

7. American Reformation Movement
   Independence Square, Suite 106, Box 138

7341 Clairemont Mesa Blvd.
San Diego, CA 92111

Publishes "On Teaching," a monthly newsletter on educational matters.

8. The Forerunner
    Maranatha Campus Ministries, Intl.
    P.O. Box 1799
    Gainsville, FL 32602

Monthly newspaper addressing issues that face collegiates and affect our nation and our world. Informative and thought-provoking journalism.

9. Hewitt Research Foundation
    P.O. Box 9
    Washougal, WA 98671-0009

Publishers of "The Parent Educator and Family Report," informing parents on matters of educational interest.

CHAPTER 17

Books recommended for further study:

1. *Addicted to Mediocrity: 20th Century Christian and the Arts*
    Franky Schaeffer
    Westchester, IL: Crossway, 1981.

An expose of Christian attitudes that have been anti-art, anti-culture, and anti-learning. A challenge to Christians to get our own house in order to influence society. (I)

2. *The Creative Gift: Essays on Art and the Christian Life*
    H. R. Rookmaaker
    Westchester, IL: Cornerstone, 1981.

Thoughtful reflection on art and freedom, history and authority, culture and creativity, by a man of international renown as a critic on art and culture. (A)

3. *Media and Arts: Journal of Christian Reconstruction, Vol. X, No. 1*

   Order from:
   Chalcedon Publications
   P.O. Box 158
   Vallecito, CA 95251

Symposium on how Christians can influence all branches of the media and the arts. (A)

Action and assistance sources·

1. Athletes in Action
   4790 Irvine Blvd. 105-325
   Irvine, CA 92714

Athletic ministry of Campus Crusade for Christ.

2. Media Spotlight
   P.O. Box 1288
   Costa Mesa, CA 92628

Publishers of "Media Spotlight," a biblical analysis of entertainment and the media. The publication's purpose is to analyze mass communications media and entertainment, as well as philosophies and ideas as manifested through religions, cults, government, education, and any other public forum.

3. Pro Athletes Outreach
   The Park
   4455 E. Camelback, Suite 270E
   Phoenix, AZ 85018

A Christian ministry to professional athletes.

4. Artists in Christian Testimony
9090 19th Street
Alta Loma, CA 91701

An organization aiming to encourage and coordinate Christian artists in expressing their Christian testimony.

CHAPTER 18

Books recommended for further study:

1. *The Biblical Basis for Modern Science*
Henry M. Morris
Grand Rapids, MI: Baker, 1984.

Brings together in a systematic, useful, and meaningful fashion key biblical insights and instructions related to all the natural sciences. (A)

2. *The Existence of God and the Beginning of the Universe*
William Lane Craig
San Bernardino, CA: Here's Life, 1979.

Shows systematically that life indeed has significance, value, and purpose but only in light of the existence of a personal God. (A)

3. *The Resourceful Earth*
Julian L. Simon and Herman Kahn, editors
New York: Basil Blackwell, 1984.

A powerful refutation of Global 2000, the report which pushes the panic button of the doomsayers. An impressive group of contributing authors document the facts about population, natural resources, pollution, and ecology. Far from predicting the death of planet Earth, their findings reassuringly suggest "a progressive improvement and enrichment of the earth's natural resource base, and of mankind's lot on Earth." (A)

4. *Intellectuals Speak Out About God*
   Ed. by Roy Abraham Varghese
   Chicago: Regnery Gateway, 1984.

A handbook for the Christian student in a secular society. Interviews with outstanding scholars in various fields of study. (A)

5. *The Ultimate Resource*
   Julian L. Simon
   Princeton: Princeton University, 1981.

Simon destroys the "We're running out of everything!" myth of the hysterical left. He shows that, though we may be running out of some resources, the earth still provides many yet untapped resources. Well-documented and highly informative. (A)

Action and assistance sources:

1. Institute of Creation Research
   2100 Greenfield Dr.
   El Cajon, CA 92021

Offering an alternative to the philosophy of naturalistic evolutionary humanism. Request list of publications and monthly newletter," Acts and Facts."

(We suggest you request from each of the following organizations a catalog of resources available.)

2. Creation Science Information Service
   137 Oak Crest Dr.
   Lafayette, LA 70503

3. Bible-Science Association, Inc.
   2911 E. 42nd Street
   Minneapolis, MN 55406

4. Creation Life Publishers
   P.O. Box 15666
   San Diego, CA 92115

5. Ex Nilio
   P.O. Box 6064
   Evanston, IL 60204

6. The Fair Education Foundation
   Rt. 2, Box 415
   Murphy, NC 28906

7. Creation Science Legal Defense Fund, Inc.
   P.O. Box 78312
   Shreveport, LA 71137